Showing and Ringcraft Explained

A Horseman's Handbook

Alison Sherred

Showing and Ringcraft Explained

with contributions from
Anne Alcock, Carol Green, Deirdre Robinson
and Marylian Watney

Arco Publishing Company, Inc.
New York

Horseman's Handbooks

TRAINING EXPLAINED
JUMPING EXPLAINED
STABLE MANAGEMENT EXPLAINED
DRESSAGE EXPLAINED
EVENTING EXPLAINED
TACK EXPLAINED

First published in Great Britain in 1978 by Ward Lock Limited, a member of the Pentos Group.

All rights reserved.

Published 1978 by Arco Publishing Company, Inc. 219 Park Avenue South, New York, N.Y. 10003

Copyright ©1978 by Ward Lock Limited

Library of Congress Cataloging in Publication Data
Sherred, Alison.
   Showing and ringcraft explained.
   (Horseman's handbook)
   1. Horses–Showing. 2. Horse–shows.
   I. Title. II. Series.
SF294.5.G73   798'.24   77–17185
ISBN 0–668–04405–5
ISBN 0–668–04410–1 pbk.

Printed in Great Britain by
T. & A. Constable Ltd, Edinburgh

Contents

1 Horse shows and classes 7

2 Behind the scenes 13

3 Horse show preparation 26

4 The Arab 34

5 The show hunter 42

6 Hunt seat equitation 48

7 Saddle seat equitation 52

8 The Jumper division 55

9 Western riding and stock seat equitation 64

10 The American Saddlebred 71

11 The Morgan 75

12 Tennessee Walkers 82

13 The Quarter Horse 85

14 The Appaloosa 88

15 Riding side-saddle 90

16 Driving at shows 93

Acknowledgments

We are grateful to the following for kindly providing photographs for this book: John Topham, Sally Anne Thompson, Bob Langrish, The Australian News and Information Services, Marie Stokes and Marian O'Sullivan.

1 Horse shows and classes

Horse shows are a part of the younger history of the United States. With the development of Southern plantations and the use of the horse for transportation and work, people rode their horses to town on market and court days. At first comparison, then organized competitions, developed. The horse was early a part of country fairs, and in the north-east one of the oldest horse shows, the Devon Country Fair in Pennsylvania, is still flourishing as one of the largest events in the country.

Today there are major shows in almost every state as well as thousands of local events. Because of the great travel distances involved, many shows have formed 'circuits' so that exhibitors coming from afar may participate in several consecutive shows within a region or state, making it worth their time and expense. Two of the most famous circuits are the traditional Fall Indoor Circuit (Harrisburg, Washington D.C., Madison Square Garden, and the Royal Winter Fair at Toronto) and the newer but very popular Winter Sunshine Circuit in Florida.

Each breed in the United States has its big event. For the hunters and jumpers (who are mostly Thoroughbred or Thoroughbred crosses), Madison Square Garden is probably still the most prestigious. Now almost all horses, not just the equitation riders, must qualify to compete there, and to be eligible for the Garden demands a high degree of excellence, with each trainer trying to produce his horses and riders in top condition in time for the big Fall show.

For the Saddlehorses, the Kentucky State Fair in Louisville is the home of the World Championships; the Morgans congregate in Northampton, Massachusetts; and the Tennessee Walkers in Shelbyville, Tennessee. The other breeds all have their own 'big ones', and there are also many large shows across the country that sponsor classes for the different breeds. Almost every area has its own major events within reach of an interested public.

The principle behind shows has remained unaltered over the centuries: to continue to improve a given type or breed. For this reason show horses should be models of their type. Without the

A Tennessee Walking Horse being put through its paces at a show.

incentive of shows, when breeders and exhibitors alike strive for perfection, standards could slacken to the detriment of the horse and of riding in general. Once a breeder or owner has won prizes and championships at leading shows he can command high prices for his animals, and in this way the future of well-bred horses and ponies is assured. It is at horse shows also that a trainer builds his reputation for producing winning-performance horses and riders. Many transactions take place at every major event.

Similarly, small shows play an important part, for they are needed as a stepping stone towards the higher echelons, and give encouragement to those embarking on showing. Without the small show, and even 'backyard' events, such people might fall by the wayside, knowing they could not compete with the established stars, and in this way potential talent would be lost.

The development of potential talent is strongly influenced by the role of local and national horse show associations. These governing and educational bodies help to set standards and rules for the guidance of exhibitors. Classes and divisions, all with their own eligibility requirements and rules are carefully devised to separate competitors according to ability, experience, or age. The intention is to provide everyone with fair competition and to avoid a situation where one horse and rider will always win and another lose because of an unfair handicap, such as a great difference in age or experience. This way a nine-year-old rider will not have to compete against a seventeen-year-old veteran, and a green four-year old horse may not have to battle a seven-year-old star unless, of course, they choose to do so in the open classes.

In a novice or 'green' class the judge will usually bear in mind the inexperience of the exhibitors either equine or human, and make some allowances for an imperfect performance, whereas in an open class a brilliant and finished performance is expected.

In 'ladies to ride' and children's classes, more emphasis will be placed on manners and suitability. The United States has classes especially for younger riders and the American horse-show scene sponsors complete divisions for amateur and junior riders. A junior must be under eighteen years of age and an amateur must be a non-professional horseman of eighteen years or older. Horse and rider age is usually determined by their status on 1 January of the current year.

The parent body of horse shows is the AHSA (American Horse Shows Association, 598 Madison Avenue, New York, NY 10022, USA). Apart from setting standards and enforcing rules, this organization sponsors educational programmes and, in giving its sanction to big events, tries to make sure that conflicts in dates do not occur.

To the casual visitor a show class may seem rather dull, and he will probably prefer the excitement of show-jumping to the show classes, with horses or ponies that seem just to follow one another around a ring. But like anything else, if that visitor can acquire some understanding of what it is all about, and begin to feel himself involved, the show class can take on new, exciting dimensions. As he learns the good points to look out for and spots the little bits of ringcraft displayed by exhibitors, the pastime takes on an all-embracing interest, especially once he finds the judge agreeing with his own ringside choice of winners! He will develop an 'eye' for a horse and find himself selecting four or five, then putting them in order of preference in his mind's eye, being greatly rewarded when this order tallies with the actual result.

One of the fascinations about showing is that so much depends on opinion. A given judge at a given time may differ totally from another one somewhere else, making it quite unlike a race, where the first past the post is always the winner. Although a really top-class horse is going to win at almost any show, he is not a machine and can have an off day like any other creature; you never know when he is going to come up against an improving youngster who may topple him from his position of supremacy. One of the most important things for an exhibitor to recognize when he enters any class is that he is submitting himself to the judge's opinion and must abide by the judge's decision. It is easy to be a winner but harder to be a graceful loser!

Once you have watched some show classes from the ringside you will see that they mostly follow a similar pattern. The riders perform the various gaits in one direction and then reverse and repeat them on the other hand. At this point the judge may have the steward (his ring assistant) line the class up before the awards are announced. Depending on the class, however, the decision may not be that simple. The judge may call his favourites into the centre, watch the rest to make sure he did not miss anyone, and then excuse those he does not like. He will then ask the remaining horses to work a little longer before he pins the class. Often at a big show, where the classes are large and competition very stiff, it is as great a thrill to 'make the cut' as it would be to win a class at a small event.

In any class it is essential to understand that the judge's decision is based upon what he sees in the two or ten minutes that a horse is in the ring. He can take into consideration only what he sees in that class, not how good or bad the horse was in another class or show. The clever exhibitor will realize this, and from the second he enters the ring until the very moment the class is pinned will show himself and his horse. All adjustments and preparation should be complete before entering so that the rider can devote all his concentration to keeping his horse ready for the judge's eye and putting on a polished performance. It is the rider's responsibility to be seen, not the judge's to find him in the crowd! Even when the line-up is called, the exhibitors should be alert and poised — so many classes have been lost at the last instant by a rider allowing his horse to rest a leg, or by his sitting sloppily.

A good exhibitor can make a mediocre horse look good, and the reverse is also true. 'Covering up' is a great part of showmanship, and the winners are often those who are best at minimizing errors and capitalizing on their strengths. If you know your horse has a fantastic trot, make sure he is in front of the judge, but if your transition to canter is a weak spot then hide away behind the other riders, taking advantage of the fact that the judge cannot take into account what he does not see. If your horse needs a swift nudge, or you need to shorten your rein, then do it behind your judge's back. You would be ill-advised, too, always to appear beside the best-moving horse in the class — better place yourself near the mediocre entries so that your own horse is a star. Generally, the biggest mistake of a novice is to get caught in the crowd; an experienced rider will keep out by himself when he wants to be seen and is continually avoiding horses that are kicking or causing trouble. Ride defensively!

Showing in halter or in-hand classes is a speciality of its own. Horse and handler turnout is all-important, but the movements that must be gone through in the arena should have been rehearsed, however simple they may be. A young horse should be used to crowds and strange sights and sounds and must behave well in the ring. The way that a horse is presented - 'stood up' - can make a tremendous difference in accentuating the good and bad points of his conformation. As in all horse show divisions, the novice exhibitor should spend a good deal of time at the ringside learning by observation.

The art of ringcraft comes only with experience. Anyone can win occasionally - the goal is to be consistently at or near the top!

2 Behind the scenes

The show ring, with all its glamour and excitement, is just the tip of the iceberg. For every minute in the spotlight, hours, days and months of preparation are involved. Not only must the horse be brought into the peak of condition physically and mentally, but he must perform his required gaits, or jump his course, with sparkle and style.

For all the work entailed, it is important that the aspiring exhibitor should start out with the right horse. After the initial purchase price it costs as much to own and show a bad horse as it does a good one. The feed, travel, veterinary fees, and horse show expenses will be the same whether the horse is a backyard animal or a national champion; so it is wise to start out with the best prospect you can afford, for the nicer the horse, the better the rewards should be for all your effort and expense.

It is assumed that by the time the rider is looking for a show horse he can ride at least adequately. It is also assumed that he has a trainer or ground person. No matter how good you may be, you need someone knowledgeable on the ground to confirm what you are feeling and to point out things which could improve your overall performance. Even Olympic-calibre riders depend heavily on the feedback they get from their trainers and other expert observers. In every other competitive sport a coach or trainer is the rule, and riding should be no exception.

Buying the right horse

Your trainer will probably take the initiative, if you ask him to do so, in helping you locate the right horse. The usual fee is a ten per cent commission from either the buyer or the seller. If you are working with a professional whom you trust, and you should be, this is usually a fair price to pay for the expertise, time and advice which are important in finding the right match of horse and rider. Suitability is the key, and while one horse might be a superstar for one kind of rider, he could fail miserably as someone else's mount.

In looking for a show horse or pony it is necessary to know what kind of competition you intend to enter. One animal might make an excellent equitation horse but a mediocre hunter: another might excel as a gymkhana and family pony but not make it as a show pony, although some are talented and tractable enough to be both.

There is often a great difference between a first horse and a show horse, and a common mistake is to get a horse that is too good, or has too much potential, for your current ability. A green horse and a novice rider are usually a poor combination, as neither has the experience to help the other. The horse may lose confidence or become confused and perform poorly, if at all, while the rider also will be slow to gain the experience and confidence needed to ride well. Often the green combination involves a lot of professional help and frustration - a situation that is both time-consuming and expensive.

A first horse should be experienced and, above all, kind. It should be willing and confident enough to jump or perform even when the rider makes mistakes. Looks are relatively unimportant but the horse must be capable of doing, at least on an intermediate level, what the rider wants to learn. An aspiring hunter and jumper exhibitor should have a mount that jumps safely and boldly and a hopeful 'gaited' horse rider should have something that will give them a feel of the correct headset and movement of a gaited horse. A mature first horse is preferable it could even be into its early teens - but it should be good enough to show and place at local fixtures to give its rider a chance to gain the experience he needs for successfully riding and showing a good horse. In purchasing a first horse it is important to realize that the rider will probably make quick progress. If a rider is jumping two-foot fences in January he may by July want a horse that can consistently jump three-foot courses.

Conformation

The good show prospect should possess a certain sparkle and animation that will make it stand out in a crowd. This 'presence' is what adds the finishing touch to the good looks and good performance of a top horse and separates the winners from the also-rans. It can be enhanced by certain tricks of the trade, but it cannot be created.

The horse should be sound, with no physical defects or tendencies that could be potential causes of lameness. He must have the looks or 'conformation' needed to succeed in his chosen sphere

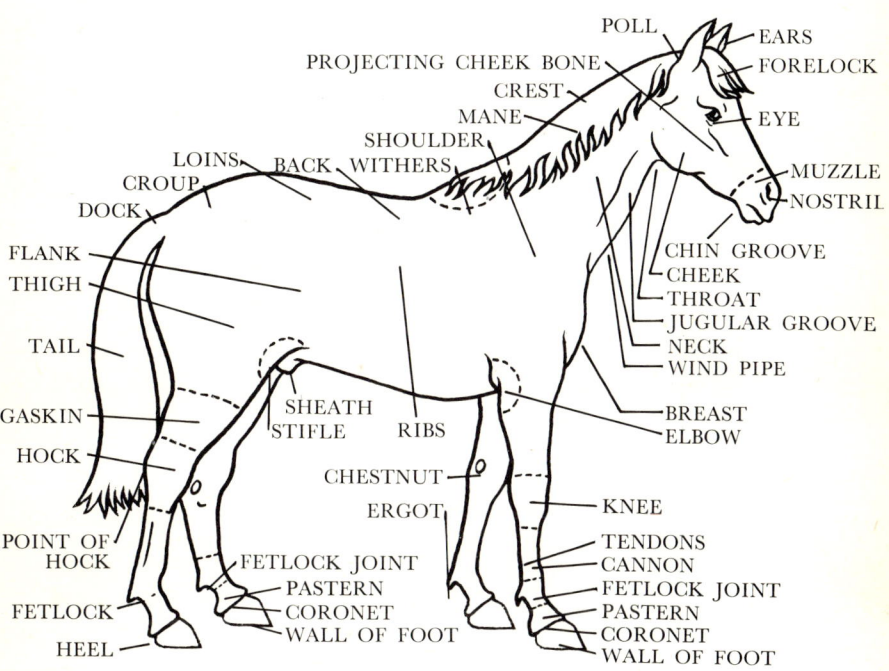

The points of the horse.

of showing. For instance, a high-headed Saddlebred with pronounced knee action is at a severe disadvantage in the American show hunter division. There are nevertheless certain conformation requirements which are basic to every show horse. A quality horse should have a small head with a good, big eye. The neck should be set on good sloping shoulders and blend well into the withers. The horse should be well coupled, with a generous girth, his hocks well let down, and the quarters strong with a nicely set tail. The feet are most important for 'no foot, no horse' is a very true saying. They should be in proportion to the size of the horse and set on to the legs by reasonably sloping pasterns. The legs should be straight, with plenty of bone in proportion to the frame of the horse. A light horse can get away with light bone so long as it is in proportion; size of bone is more important for horses with a harder working life ahead of them, such as hunters, eventers, and racehorses. When you are thinking of buying a horse, a complete and thorough examination by a reputable veterinarian is essential. For an expensive animal X-rays may be advisable.

It is a pleasure to see a fine coat, rich in colour, the mane and tail also fine in texture. The quality horse has small chestnuts and ergots, the overall picture being one of superiority and refinement. Although the perfect horse is rarely found, the total picture should be pleasing and the animal's potential or achievements as close to your ideal as possible.

Way of going

Action, or 'way of going', is important to every show horse, but particularly for those showing under saddle or on the flat only. Action will vary depending upon the type of horse. A show hunter

Opposite An Arab champion with the classic features of the breed, the short back, level croup, high-set tail and fine head set on an elegant neck.

Overleaf top Exercising before the show is essential to ensure that the horse is warmed up and responsive to the rider.

Overleaf below If the horse has been thoroughly and regularly groomed, his coat, mane and tail will be in good condition and a polish with a stable rubber and body brush before the show, should suffice.

or hack should move very close to the ground with a long, free stride, while a gaited horse such as the American Saddlebred, or other breeds such as the Hackney, should display high knee action. All horses destined for the show ring should move straight, with the hind legs following the track of the corresponding foreleg. Except in performance classes over fences or working cattle, deviations from straightness of action are usually heavily penalized. A good mover in any division should be really free in the shoulder and carry his hocks well under himself.

Stable management

To produce or keep a horse in top show condition, meticulous stable management is required. Feed, shoeing, veterinary attention, grooming, and exercise or training are the five basics. They are discussed in detail in *Stable Management Explained* in this series, but a short review is in order here.

Feeding Every stable has its own feeding practices according to location and climate. Care must be taken to feed only top quality grains or mixes and to adhere to a strict schedule. A sudden change in feed, either of type or quantity, can cause severe disorders. Any change should be made gradually, and careful attention paid to the horse's condition. Some horses get too hot on a high oats ration and may fare better on some combination of grains or pellets. 'Good doers' are easy to keep and require little to maintain their energy and looks, while fussy feeders are difficult. All horses should have some sort of mineral salt block and many will do well to have a vitamin or mineral supplement with their feed. Clean water should be available at all times, although a horse should never be allowed to drink too much water immediately after a

Previous page Equipment for showing, boxing and stabling should be kept clean and in good condition.
Opposite Hoof oil, painted on the hooves with a small brush will improve the appearance and condition of the feet.

feed or when they are hot from work. It is essential to understand the science of feeding, as each horse is an individual and diet is one of the most important aspects of maintaining your horse in peak condition.

Veterinary attention Even the best diet is to no avail unless co-ordinated with a rigid worming programme. Depending upon location and lifestyle, most horses will need worming at least three times a year; twice is an absolute minimum. Many top show stables perform some kind of worming routine every two months. Every horse should receive tetanus vaccinations and you should consult your veterinarian about inoculations against other diseases. Horses that are frequently on the road and exposed to other animals should receive whatever preventative shots are recommended. In many places in the United States an annual Coggins test is required. This controversial diagnostic test is intended to prevent the spread of Swamp Fever. If a horse does not seem to be in as good condition as he should be, the first thing to check for is worms, the second to see if his teeth need floating so he can more easily chew and digest his food, and the third may be to resort to some blood tests and find out if there are any vitamin or mineral deficiencies or other disorders. Even lack of salt in the horse's diet can have a serious effect.

Shoeing A healthy horse is no use unless he is sound. One of the biggest preventative measures against lameness is frequent hoof care by a good farrier. Even a horse who is laid up for a period should receive frequent attention. An unshod hoof needs to be trimmed regularly to maintain correct angles in the foot and leg, and to keep the hoof itself healthy. If the hoof is allowed to grow too long, the possibility of bone and tissue damage is increased, as concussion will be absorbed at a strange angle throughout the leg; an over-long hoof when shod runs the risk of corns and other foot discomforts caused by the shoe pinching. A good farrier is essential - a poor one can do more harm than good. One nail misplaced, or a foot cut too short, can cause severe lameness. An experienced farrier may be able to correct some faults in a horse's

Here the farrier is in the process of fitting the heated shoe to the foot.

action: techniques such as rolling the toe or weighting the shoe, judiciously used, may enhance a horse's natural way of going. Different shoes can be useful in various types of competition: some shoes for example, are designed to allow for the addition of studs to help over wet ground. As a rule, most horses will need shoeing every four to seven weeks, although this varies according to location and the time of year.

Grooming To see real results from grooming, it must be practised as a routine over an extended period. The hard work put in while shaggy winter coats abound will not really show until the horse loses the winter coat and his summer shine appears. Daily grooming not only losens the dirt, it also massages the skin and oil glands. Brushing removes the dirt, and a stable rubber or towel, perhaps slightly damped, wipes away surface dust. The nose, eyes, mouth, dock and genital area should be frequently sponged clean and it is essential to a healthy hoof that it be picked out regularly. Dry hooves may require the application of oil or grease. An important part of the grooming procedure is to keep an eye on the horse's condition and to inspect for cuts, wounds, or the development of skin conditions.

Exercise If the horse is healthy and sound, his exercise or training has a good foundation. As for the amount or type of work needed, each animal is an individual - some thrive on hard work, others get too fit to ride pleasurably, and some get bored or stale. It is up to the trainer and rider to work out a suitable programme for each animal. With a novice rider, the rider's training programme may also have to be taken into account, to allow for his own progress and ability to ride and show their horse!

In general, each horse's programme must be consistent but at the same time varied. The rider must always make sure that his demands are understood; to produce a responsive, relaxed horse the signals he is asked to respond to are consistently clear, and always enforced if not immediately obeyed. An angry or sour animal has often been created by an inefficient and inconsistent rider who constantly makes unclear or unreasonable demands on his mount. Along with a consistent programme where the horse understands what is wanted and is never overfaced or asked to perform tasks that are above his present level of training, an important ingredient to successful training is variety. One of the biggest challenges with a horse in the midst of a heavy show season is to keep the sparkle in his performance. A routine gone through too often may be technically accurate but will lose its animation.

To keep a horse eager to work is again an individual matter. As a rule, a green horse, by the very fact of his inexperience, will find daily training more interesting than would a show veteran who thinks he knows it all. A young horse may be best brought along by short daily routines that sometimes introduce new ideas, but consistently revise, while the veteran may need only occasional schooling sessions to sharpen him up. Almost every horse will enjoy a hack as a change of work, and while lessons can be put into practice the more relaxed exercise will do both horse and rider good. Even a change in location can add a little interest to an old routine and help the horse to learn to keep his attention on his rider and not on new surroundings. Work up and down hills helps to build muscle and balance. More about riding and training is discussed in another volume in this series, *Training Explained*.

Pre-show training

A winning performance in the ring is marked by a sense of smoothness and presence and an apparent lack of effort. The horse should appear to perform on his own, without the rider's aid, and to slide from one gait to another with ease. Everything should be fluid and graceful. Perfection of performance can only be attained by practice, but for most horses the wise trainer will rarely put together the whole thing until the day of the show. The different movements and transitions will be rehearsed, the manoeuvres or jumps gone over and over, but the whole course or class routine will be run through only occasionally to ensure that it fits together smoothly. This way the horse does not learn to anticipate, and his interest in his work will be maintained on show day.

Rhythm is basic to any good show. An evenness and fluidity must always be present - the horse should not shorten his stride in the corners, or keep varying the height of his action. He must respond to the slightest leg and hand aids and never lose his balance in the transitions. From the moment he enters the ring until the prizes are given, he must be at his best. The ideal is for your horse to look like a lion but behave like a lamb.

3 Horse show preparation

Apart from the extended and gradual conditioning and training that is the background to the show season, there is a certain amount of direct pre-show preparation that every exhibitor must go through. This will vary depending upon whether you travel alone or with a big stable and whether you are exhibiting mostly at one-day shows or at week-long events.

Early in the year a tentative show schedule can be arranged. Priorities must be established for each horse, and care taken that horse and rider, should they prove successful, will not be upgraded until they are ready. It is essential to be absolutely familiar with all status and eligibility rules of your governing associations so that you do not, inadvertently, move your horse into a new division until he is ready. Sometimes a horse's career must be planned several years in advance.

Once you have planned what shows or circuits you will compete in, you must ensure that your training schedule will produce your horse at the correct level of performance. The horse must never be overfaced, particularly not in the show ring, and should always be completely competent at home before he is asked to perform at a show.

It is a great advantage for a young horse to attend a couple of shows as a spectator only, to allow him to become familiar with the whole show atmosphere. Only when he is relaxed in strange surroundings will he be able to perform his best. At his first few shows as an exhibitor he should be entered in the simplest classes only - and three a day is usually enough for a baby. The aim is to make showing an enjoyable, not frightening or tiring, experience.

Once your show schedule has been decided upon it is necessary to send your entries in by the deadlines. Late entries may be accepted at an additional fee or in some cases rejected altogether.

If the show is at some distance from your home it may be necessary to make overnight accommodations for both you and your horse well in advance. In addition to the entry fees, AHSA shows require a small drug fee from each competitor. These funds are used to finance routine testing of various winners as a precaution against the use of stimulants, depressants, and other illegal substances. As certain legal medicines may act as masking agents they too are not allowed and whenever you need to administer medicine within a few days of show time do check carefully with your veterinarian that it will not leave traces in the system that could still be present, and possibly illegal, on show day. The painkiller 'bute' is legal in the United States. This is a controversial point, as while it is useful in relieving temporary soreness (a bruise, for example) it could also allow an animal who is genuinely injured, and should be resting, to work and perhaps cause further damage.

Stabling

If you will be stabling your horse overnight at a show, be sure that bedding is provided - if not, you will have to plan to take your own. Often, the first night's bedding is provided, but you must purchase or bring with you the extra needed for a four- or five-day stay. Stalls may not have latches, so plan to bring your own locks and, of course, you should count on bringing your own water buckets and feed tubs. Don't forget mucking-out tools and, if you are renting an additional stall as a tack room, your portable saddle racks and other fittings. A tack-cleaning hook is always useful, as are conveniences like a lamp, an electric water heater, and a coffee pot if electricity is available. A flashlight or torch is always handy Many big stables fit out their tack rooms in a décor worthy of a living room, and it provides a comfortable retreat or headquarters while at the show - often doubling up as the night watchman's or groom's bedroom! If you are travelling with a stable, most of the horse's accommodation and travel arrangements will be handled by your trainer or manager. It is wisest to bring the feed your horse is used to unless you are certain you can purchase it at the show. Avoid the common water trough for your horse, as it is an invitation to disease.

During the show season your trunk will become your travelling tack room. Equip it well! Along with all your regular requirements you will want to carry spares in case of loss or breakage. Extra buckles, lead ropes and reins are never regretted. It is a good idea to keep a checklist in your tack trunk lid so as not to forget an important item. Basic tools like a hammer and nails can be indispensable.

Travelling routines

If you are hauling your own trailer or driving your own box or truck, it is a heavy responsibility to make certain that all brakes, lights, locks, suspensions, hitches and other details are in excellent repair. The horse should be well protected for travelling with wraps or boots, hock or knee caps and maybe a head protector. If the horse is to wear any special equipment on a trip, make sure that he first becomes accustomed to it in his own stable. A disadvantage of some travelling gear is that it can be uncomfortably warm on a hot day. The business of loading a young horse should not be left until the day he has to be transported to a show; he should be used to short trips and loading and unloading before he is ever taken in a van to a horse show. It is as much a part of his

The tail bandage. Here you see the first stage, notice the end in the groom's hand.

The end of the tail bandage is folded over the first loop and then wound round.

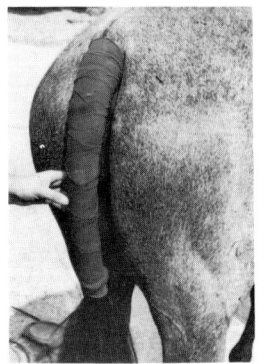

The finished tail bandage.

Travelling boots are a useful alternative to the stable bandage, to protect the legs while travelling.

training as any other exercise and it should be well-rehearsed on his home-ground beforehand. Make the whole experience of loading as pleasant as possible for the young horse: position the trailer in such a way as to get maximum light inside, open all windows and ventilators for light and air and reward your horse, once inside the trailer, with a small feed. Always walk the horse slowly and calmly to the trailer, without rushing him, and remain close to his shoulder until he is safely inside. In this way the horse will have no reason to fear loading or travelling.

Equipment for showing

The turnout of horse and rider in the show ring is all-important 'Handsome is as handsome does' is true, but first impressions are lasting and a judge cannot help but be heavily influenced by appearances, for that is certainly part of the game. Fortunately at small shows and novice events, neatness and cleanliness is the rule, but as you and your horse progress, a custom fit is essential. Often, by careful shopping, a subtle but striking outfit can be arranged economically but it is sometimes necessary to go to considerable expense to acquire the right equipment. Fit is the prime concern for comfort as well as looks. In general it is better to stay conservative in colour choice. Before embarking on a spending spree, become thoroughly familiar with the options and requirements of your show divisions. At larger shows attire may change for the evening or afternoon classes. If your budget is limited, buy classic outfits and colours that do not change with the yearly fad. Often there is a good second-hand market of quality equipment, particularly in children's sizes.

The one item that should never be scrimped upon is your saddle. It is worth going overboard on this purchase to get exactly the right fit for both you and your horse, as a good saddle can enhance performance considerably and a bad one really hinder it. The horse must be absolutely comfortable in order to perform his

An original Hermes saddle, designed for 'close contact' it places the rider in a very well-balanced position.

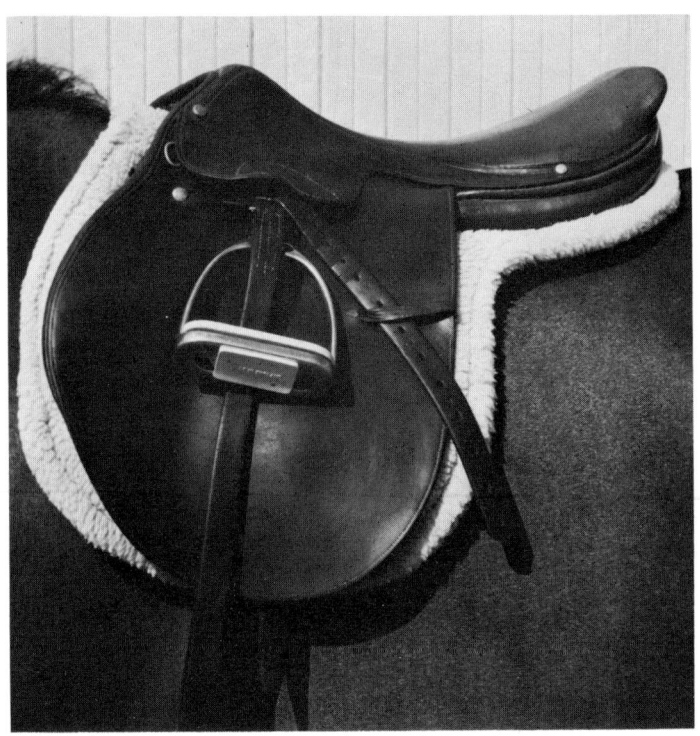

best. It is never a mistake to buy quality leather as it lasts well, has good resale value, and there is the risk of cheap leather breaking without warning.

It goes without saying that you, your horse and all your equipment and tack should be meticulously presented. Tack will need to be wiped over after every class and all metal parts should be polished and shining.

Grooming before a show

Assuming that a faithful grooming routine has been practised regularly, pre-show or pre-class grooming presents no problem. The horse's clean coat should be wiped over with a towel to remove any dust. Feet should be oiled or blackened depending upon the current fashion. If there are flies about, it is essential to use an insect repellent, as no horse looks its best when fidgeting and tossing because of pests. You may want to spray a sheen on the coat or

Grooming kit. From left, top row: water brush, tail bandage, mane and tail comb, scissors (for trimming the feathers on the heels), two sponges, hoof pick, hoof oil. Bottom row: body brush, metal curry comb, wisp and dandy brush.

put a little Vaseline or baby oil around the eyes. Hair conditioner can help the tail and whitener can brighten your horse's socks, should he have any. The mane and tail should be braided, combed, or fixed according to the type of class, and as close to your class as possible to ensure that they are as neat and impressive-looking as can be. A clever braiding job can make a short neck look longer by using many miniature braids, and a well-shaped tail can accentuate or improve the hindquarters. If you do give your horse a shampoo bath, it should be done infrequently and never too close to show day as it will remove the oils and shine from the coat. A pure water rinse will normally be sufficient, and will not remove the oils.

Trimming

The finishing touch to a nice turnout of horse and rider is good trimming. Again, this is an art, and like braiding should be practised long in advance of the show season. The usual procedure is to trim excess hair from the muzzle, under the head, eyes, ears, poll, fetlocks, pastern, and coronet areas. A good job will be invisible: it

Tail pulling with a comb.

accentuates a fine horse's features and can minimize the coarseness of a heavier animal.

Showing procedures

Before the rider actually shows the horse he should be thoroughly familiar with ring procedure, having observed many other classes before first competing himself. As you are in the ring for a short period only, it is essential to allow yourself plenty of time to get yourself turned out and warmed up. Many classes have been lost because an exhibitor did not allow himself enough time to prepare adequately. After the class the horse should be thoroughly cared for, and at the end of a hard day a liniment wash-down can be a welcome relief for tired muscles.

This behind-the-scenes part of showing is half the fun of it - no one is a consistent winner without faithful homework and preparation!

4 The Arab

Until recently a great many misguided people thought the mere fact that they owned a pure-bred Arabian was sufficient qualification to appear in the show ring, regardless of whether or not it was a good show specimen. Happily things are now changing: Arab owners are becoming educated both from the point of view of riding and producing a better class of animal, and taking much

An Arab stallion, strong, hardy and outstandingly sound, it is perhaps the most beautiful breed.

more care about the correct schooling and presentation of it. The judges, too, are more aware of the basic needs of the ridden Arab and there is less tendency to put up the one with the best conformation over the better schooled, but perhaps plainer, animal. Arab breeders and judges are becoming more and more sophisticated and there are strong Arab divisions at many major shows as well as large regional all-Arabian shows.

Breeders who have the welfare and future of the Arabian at heart are encouraging people to geld all but the very best colts. Arab blood has, over time, been infused to improve many other breeds. One would do well to remember that many Thoroughbreds trace back to the Byerley Turk, the Godolphin Arabian and the Darley Arabian. The genuine desert Arabian was exceptionally hardy, fleet of foot, and possessed enormous stamina. Today's Arabian is a graceful and co-ordinated creature, unusually alert and quick on its feet, and compact in build. The back is short with a fairly level croup and high-set tail; the head, upon an elegant neck, is dish-faced and delicate, with large, wide-set eyes and flaring nostrils in a tiny muzzle; the ears are intelligent and point towards each other. An average horse is fairly small, usually standing between 14.1 and 15.1 hands.

To produce your Arab correctly for the show ring he must first have been thoroughly schooled in the basic principles that are expected of all horses. He must go forward with impulsion and enthusiasm under control, with correct rhythm in all his gaits, and he must also have the correct bend. All these things he must learn to do in a snaffle bridle before you ever consider putting on a pelham. The trot is the Arab's outstanding gait, but before you can ask for true extension you must have established a really good working trot. This is very important, since many otherwise good horses tend to be either high behind or have bad hocks. With correct schooling these weaknesses can be improved. Horses that are trotting as fast as they can lay their legs to the ground, with their noses stuck in the air and their hocks flying out behind them, may look spectacular to the uninitiated but they are actually out of rhythm and lacking in balance, making for unlevel paces and a jarring, unbalanced ride.

The governing Arabian body is the international Arabian Horse Association (PO Box 4502, 224 East Olive Avenue, Burbank, California 91503) which has over 175 member associations scattered throughout the United States and Canada. The Association awards Legion of Merit degrees to outstanding Arabs and half-Arabs who have earned the required number of points, supports horse shows and sponsors many educational endeavours. In order to show in the Arabian Division, all American horses must be registered with the Arabian Horse Club Registry of America in Barrington, Illinois which was founded in 1908.

Arab division

Show divisions for Arabs are separated into English and Western classes, and park ('showy') or pleasure events. Except in hunter, jumper and cutting classes horses should show in full — that is, unbraided — mane and tail. Unnatural methods such as gingering, tail setting, rollers and other action devices are prohibited. Horses must be shown with a fairly short foot (maximum length of toe is 4½in) and a fairly average weight shoe.

The park classes are where the Arabian's free way of moving is really put to the test. The park trot demands tremendous freedom of shoulder and great reach and lift with the hind legs. The front legs may either be raised at the knee or just greatly extended, and the hocks should really lift and drive, well under the horse, in floating co-ordination with the front. Posting is not required and many professionals bounce to this gait. At no time should form be sacrificed for speed.

One of the most popular spectator classes is the 'formal combination', where park horses perform first in harness and then under saddle. Handlers take pride in the speed with which they

Opposite Washing the horse's tail with a bucket of warm water, a large sponge and special shampoo.

Overleaf The tail should be carefully rinsed in a bucket of clean warm water.

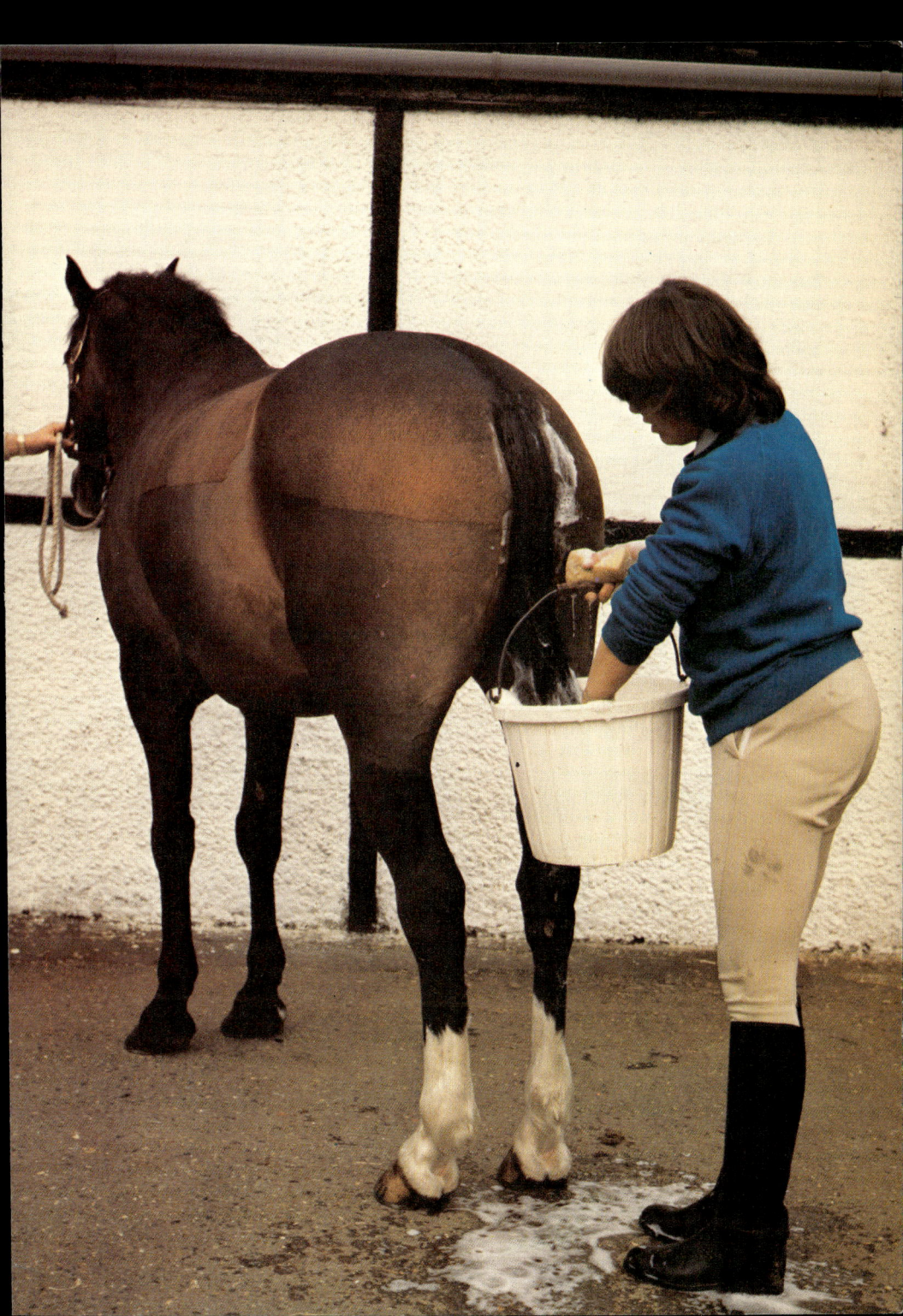

make the change of tack, with the help of their 'header' or ground man, in the middle of the arena. The most colourful classes are the native costume events. Exhibitors arrayed in various desert regalia with colourful tassels and flowing capes, perform at the walk, canter and hand gallop. Appointments are judged for twenty-five per cent, and performance and manners count seventy-five per cent — a class that recalls the Arab's origins.

There is also an active Arabian Cutting Horse Association and the cutting horses compete, along with the pleasure, park, costume, stock, hunter, jumper, trail, driving and halter horses at the highlight of every year, the Arabian and half-Arabian United States National Championships horse show held on alternate years at Albuquerque, New Mexico and Louisville, Kentucky.

Previous page The tail is dried by shaking and flicking it to remove the surplus water.

Opposite Washing the horse's white socks will enhance his appearance for the show ring.

5 The show hunter

The American show hunter is judged almost entirely upon performance, except in classes designated as 'Model' or 'Conformation' events. The art of showing hunters has become a refined skill and at the top shows only a truly excellent combination of horse and rider can win.

In a Working Hunter class each horse is usually required to jump a series of eight to ten fences that will include one in-and-out (two jumps placed at a related distance of one or two strides from each other) and at least one change of direction. The fences should be of natural material although some shows, for lack of knowledge or jumps, use the type of obstacles found in the show-jumping ring, such as brightly painted poles, barrels, diagonal slats, etc. Normal hunter-type fences might include the following: a coop, a wall, a gate, hay bales, brush, toronto and perhaps, at a larger show, a bank.

Above all else, a show hunter must be a good jumper. Unlike the jumper division, where it is only the horse's ability to clear the obstacles that matters, the hunter is being judged on his style, use of his body, and consistency. It is easy enough for the casual spectator to pick out the consistent and easy-going horse - the one who leaves the ground for every fence at approximately the same distance from it and who moves smoothly between his fences - but it takes the expert to distinguish the really good jumper. This good jumper is very 'free in the shoulder' and capable of really snapping his knees up even when he has to take off very close to the fence. In the air, the horse should round his back, pulling his hocks and hind legs neatly up and reaching forward and down with the head and neck. The most important factor in good jumping is the use of the forearm and knee: they should be well lifted so that a line extended from the elbow to the knee would point skyward. The best jumpers also tuck their lower legs neatly and and hold their knees evenly over the top of the fence. The worst jumper is the one who hangs his knees or drops a leg. These two faults are serious and will usually eliminate a horse from the ribbons even if most of his other fences are superb. Both hanging (which means letting the knees, not just the lower legs, hang down) and extreme unevenness in the front legs, could result in the horse hitting the fence on his knees or above and having a nasty fall. Jumping form is improved not so much by jumping courses as by working a horse through various exercises and gymnastics (such as short combinations), which teach him how best to negotiate obstacles comfortably.

Except on an outside course, where jumps may be set at random distances and lines between fences be optional, striding

Champion hunter 'Sure Now' is not only a good jumper but a fine example of the Appaloosa breed.

(the number of strides the horse takes between two fences on a straight line) is very important. Course designers usually assume an average stride of 12ft and allow approximately 6ft each for take-off and landing. This means that a distance of 72ft between two fences will ride correctly in five strides. How easily this is done depends on several factors: how your horse meets the first fence, the footing, what part of the course the distance is on (a horse will find it easier to extend towards the end of a course, or heading home), and whether he is naturally long or short-strided. This is where the rider's judgement plays an important role. An experienced rider will know whether to move his horse on, steady it, or just maintain its pace or length of stride. Some riders are born with a naturally good eye, while others must acquire one through constant practice. Detailed advice on training over a variety of jumps and obstacles can be found in *Jumping Explained.* For anyone showing over fences, practice is important as only through doing it again and again can you maintain and improve your eye, timing and rhythm.

From the moment the hunter starts the course and makes the preliminary warm-up circle, rhythm is important. In the first circle the rider should establish the rhythm (evenness of one stride to the next) and pace that he intends to keep throughout the round. After every fence is jumped the horse must come back to the original rhythm. If the horse lands slightly out of balance usually a little on the forehand with the stride too forward and long, the rider must re-establish balance by helping to shift the weight back over the hocks, the position from which the horse can jump best. This rebalance is usually accomplished by a slight check with the hand accompanied by a supporting leg and shift backwards of the rider's upper body: done well, it is so subtle as to be barely noticeable, and should not interfere in the least with a fluid round.

Hunter divisions

The AHSA has many hunter divisions and, along with entering in classes at local unrecognized shows, a thoughtful trainer can produce each young horse in exactly the right manner. Most horses start their first year in AHSA shows in non-point classes (that is, not counting towards year-end high score awards) such as the pre-green and novice divisions. Pre-green is for any horse who has never shown over fences in an AHSA show and is not entered in any jumping classes over 3ft 6in fences at these shows, and novice is for one who has not won three blues at an AHSA show in hunter classes. Fence heights in these divisions are modest, 3ft and 3ft 3in respectively, and it is a good introduction to showing over fences. The following year, the horse will usually move to the first year green division where the fences are 3ft 6in, the subsequent year to second year (3ft 9in) and then on to the open or regular working hunter division (4ft). Often, once a horse starts in the first year division he will also be shown in the junior hunter or amateur division (both 3ft 6in). It is not unusual to see the same horse, if it has recently been purchased, ridden by a professional in the first year division and then by his owner in the junior or amateur classes. Fence heights may be a little lower than those quoted here at smaller or local shows. A popular division for some of the novice juniors is the children's hunter class, with fences at (3ft).

It is very important not to show your horse in an AHSA show unless you intend to upgrade him. Even if you enter only one pre-green, or first or second year class, in a season you will have moved your horse up a division for the next year.

Overall, apart from the all-important jumping style, the judge is looking for a fluid round, and the rider should aim to make any necessary adjustments as smoothly as possible. The judge will mark his impressions of every fence on his card in his own 'shorthand' and it is permissible in both hunter and hunt seat equitation classes to request permission to see the judge's cards after a class, although the judge has the option of refusal. Some of the bigger shows have been trying the open judging system, where each of two or three judges post their scores and the final figure is an average of the different numbers. This open judging system, which appeals greatly to spectators as it allows them to follow each class better, is frequently used in the hunter classics.

The classics have become increasingly popular events at the bigger shows. The format of these competitions varies slightly from place to place, but most require that every horse perform an original round and then the top horses, perhaps twelve or so, are asked to return and perform again. Every round is awarded a numerical score (either from an individual judge or, more often, the average from a panel) and the winner is the contestant with the highest average from the two rounds. Obviously, the winner must be capable of a really consistent performance, and as good prize money is offered these events draw many top horses into competitions together. Courses may be set at a stiff 4ft 6in and strongly favour a bold, long-striding, jumping horse.

Before the results on any hunter class are officially announced, the top horses (usually five at a small show, up to eight at a bigger event) and two reserves (four in a conformation class) are asked to jog in. Jogging in consists of trotting your horse in-hand past the judge so that he or she can make a quick soundness check. Before jogging in the stirrups should be run up and reins taken over the horse's head. The original rider does not have to jog their horse in, but every horse must be wearing its original bridle to get pinned. If a horse displays signs of unsoundness he will be eliminated and the lower horses moved up, placing one of the reserves in the ribbons.

Classes for hunters under saddle are usually held towards the end of a show, and require that horses perform as a group on the flat only at a walk, trot and canter with one change of direction. Except in green hunter classes, eight horses at a time are asked to hand gallop in one direction. Light contact is suggested and the judge is usually looking for the best movers in the class, relaxed and responsive, who cover ground easily.

A rapidly growing division, already enormous in certain parts of the country, are the pony hunter classes. The ponies are judged very similarly to the working hunters but greater emphasis is placed upon suitability of pony to rider, and extreme speed is penalized. A pony must at all times (except in breeding classes) be handled by a junior rider, that is, a rider who has not reached his eighteenth birthday. Where the division is split into three sections, ponies between 13.2 and 14.2 hands will jump 3ft fences; ponies between 12.2 and 13.2 hands will jump 2ft 6in; and those under 12.2 hands 2ft 3in. An official measurement card, issued by the AHSA, is required at AHSA shows. At smaller shows there is often just a large and small division, with the small and medium-sized ponies combined. Some shows offer a green pony division also. A popular event every year is the national AHSA hunter pony competition. To be eligible a pony must have won a championship or reserve at an 'A' show in the qualifying year. The competition is judged one-third on conformation, one-third under saddle, and one-third over fences.

6   Hunt seat equitation

Hunt seat equitation has evolved in the United States during the last ten to fifteen years into a highly competitive sport. Formerly, a rider who maintained a classic position and sat pretty on a horse could win, but today juniors are almost always really capable riders with a lot of feel for their horses. To handle the advanced equitation courses now used in Medal, Maclay, and USET (United States Equestrian Team - sponsored) classes, a rider must be really thinking and feeling to turn in a winning round.

The usual horsemanship ladder is to start in local horse shows or in the maiden, novice or limit divisions (for riders who have not won one, three, or six blues respectively) of the larger events. Each regional horse show association has its own rules governing eligibility for various classes. Under AHSA rules, if you win a blue in maiden on the flat at an AHSA show you are no longer eligible for maiden flat classes but may still show maiden over fences; if you win over fences, however, you can no longer compete in maiden flat or fences classes.

It is expected, though not required, that riders show in appropriate classes, and here the trainer's, rider's or parents' discretion must be exercised. It is foolish for a child who is not even being placed in novice classes to go ahead and compete in Medal and Maclay. Although sometimes excusable for the sake of experience, it does clutter up the advanced classes, put unnecessary wear on the horse, and make for a longer day for everyone. It is usual for most juniors to be simultaneously competing in the pony, children's or junior hunter divisions so, unless they are among the lucky few with both an equitation horse and a hunter or jumper, their horses have a busy enough day without being entered in unnecessary classes.

The Alfred B. Maclay finals are held every year at Madison

The champion hunter 'Celebrate' competing at the Phoenix A to Z horse show, the rider is without stirrups in the Hunt Seat Equitation class.

Square Garden, while the AHSA Medal ride-offs are held at a designated show such as the Pennsylvania National at Harrisburg. For both finals there are elimination ride-offs in the morning and then the top contestants are called back in the afternoon for further tests. The testing is thorough, and over the years many Medal and Maclay winners have gone on to become Olympic riders or top professional trainers.

While the Medal qualifying classes are held mainly over fences, the Maclay classes require that the better riders also return to work on the flat. The USET class is held over a jumper-type course and also requires the top competitors to return for a thorough workout on the flat. Unlike all other classes at AHSA shows, in the USET class the workoff tests are not restricted to those listed in the Hunt Seat section of the AHSA Rulebook. The Rulebook tests are as follows:

Test 1: Back.
     2: Gallop and pull up.
     3: Figure eight at trot.
     4: Figure eight at canter, simple change of lead.
     5: Jump low fences at walk and trot as well as canter.
     6: Pull up between fences except in a combination.
     7: Jump fences on a figure-eight course.
     8: Ride without stirrups.
     9: Dismount and mount.
    10: Jump serpentine course with lead change.
    11: Figure eight at canter, flying change of lead.
    12: Change leads down centre of ring, simple changes.
    13: Serpentine at trot and/or canter, simple or flying changes as requested.
    14: Change horses or ride strange horse.
    15: Canter on the counter lead.
    16: Half turn on the forehand or haunches.
    17: Demonstration ride of approximately one minute.

Although it is technically the rider who is being judged, there is no doubt that an excellent horse is needed to win at the better shows; a good horse will help his rider to turn in a better round. It is quite an art to match horse and rider for equitation events. A quiet rider might look best on a bold and sensitive horse, while the more aggressive jockey could be well-matched by a less sensitive but capable mount. If ability and temperament are a prime concern, physical attributes are also a consideration in buying an equitation horse. A short-legged rider with a long torso will look much better on a narrow-bodied, tall horse; and a long-legged rider on a bigger-barrelled animal. As the overall impression is so important in horsemanship events, it is a disadvantage to a rider not to be mounted on a horse that complements him well and presents a picture of total harmony. Of course, whatever the looks, the performance counts most of all and the horse must be well trained and obedient as well as a good looker.

As in all equitation events, clothes either enhance or detract from the hunt seat rider's appearance. If it is at all possible, the rider competing in advanced classes should be wearing custom boots and an excellent fit in jacket and breeches. Gloves are also essential.

Whatever the level of horsemanship a rider is competing at, the goal should be to produce the best results possible from the horse, to be effective, while still maintaining poise, elegance, and position. You can no longer just sit pretty and win - you must also think, feel and ride!

7 Saddle seat equitation

The saddle-seat style of riding in the United States is used to show off the sparkling action and animated way of going of several breeds. The style is very popular in the riding and showing of American Saddlebreds, Morgans, Arabs and Walking horses.

The saddle itself is a cut-back variety with straight (as opposed to hunt seat's forward) flaps and no leg padding or knee rolls. Its design is intended to enhance and encourage the natural action of the animated show horse. Being cut-back and

Martin Cockriel, wearing a traditional saddle suit in showing the five-gaited American Saddlebred stallion, 'Spellcaster'.

straight-flapped, it allows for maximum freedom of the shoulder and does not interfere with the high head carriage of these horses.

The development of a good show saddle horse, whatever the breed, requires careful training. The novice spectator may be struck by the glamour and speed of the flashy animals performing their various gaits in saddle horse and park classes, but the experienced eye can quickly distinguish the potentially great horses. High action is an asset to any of these show horses, but it must never be developed at the expense of good form. The horse that is magnificent with its front end, reaching and snapping high above the ground, must still be balanced, consistent, and holding a good head carriage. If the front end has extremely high action, then so must the hocks, and the hind end should be carried under the horse for true balance, not trailed behind. The overall picture cannot be one of symmetry and balance unless the head is correctly carried.

Saddle seat equitation classes are also a training ground for riders. Although the American Saddlebred is by far the most popular mount in the top ranks of equitation competition, being the ultimate in refinement and showiness, the Morgan has also carried many young riders to important equitation wins.

Equitation classes

The equitation classes are usually divided into three main age groups: ten and under; eleven to thirteen; and fourteen to seventeen. Each show varies according to regional associations. The three major events, held across the nation, are the AHSA Saddle Seat Medal, the National Horse Show, Good Hands, qualifying classes and the UPHA (Professional Horseman's Association) Medal class. The finals for the two medal classes are held at the American Royal Horse Show in Kansas City, and that for the 'Good Hands' class at Madison Square Garden.

As the ride-offs for these major events are in the fall, it usually allows enough time for the horse to have a short rest after a hectic summer schedule. Both horse and rider have then to be brought carefully back to the peak of condition and readiness.

The partnership of horse and rider is, again, vital in equitation classes, but the horse and its performance are more essential to the rider's chances. Riders are judged on basic position and motion at gaits, aids, skill and showmanship and ability to show their mount to its best advantage. Although the judges will be comparing the riders, not their mounts, they cannot help but be influenced by the horses. If two riders are demonstrating equal skill and style, then in all likelihood the one on the flashier mount will win because they present an added sparkle or presence — the winning touch. The better the horse, the better the rider will be able to show it.

The usual procedure is for the judge to ask the class to ride round the ring in both directions at a walk, trot, and canter and then, once the class has lined up or gathered at one end of the ring, perhaps to ask for additional tests from a few, or possibly all, the exhibitors. In the AHSA Medal class, for instance, the top four competitors are required to do two or more individual tests. As the tests must be chosen from among those listed in the AHSA Rulebook the fully prepared exhibitor will have rehearsed the possibilities thoroughly at home. The ten and under rider can probably expect to be asked for tests 1, 2, 3 or 4 (pick up reins; rein back; performance on the rail; performance around the ring), while the eleven to thirteen year-olds might also be asked for test 5, 6 or 7 (figure eight at a trot; figure eight at a canter with a simple lead change; serpentine at the trot and/or canter with simple lead changes). The remaining tests are permitted in the Open, fourteen to eighteen, and Medal classes. They are: Test 8: Change of lead down centre of ring (simple changes); 9: Ride without stirrups; 10: Demonstration ride, one minute; 11: Change horses; 12: Ride a horse supplied by the show committee.

Obviously, the more advanced equitation rider should have a predetermined demonstration ride. It should be simple enough to come off smoothly, but daring enough really to show off the rider and horse. At no point can form be sacrificed for speed or sparkle, but the student who is always underriding his horse to avoid making mistakes will rarely beat the true horseman who takes some calculated risks to bring out its best performance.

8 The Jumper Division

Jumper classes in America are rapidly making their way into the public eye. Although they have yet to receive the news coverage and public support that European events are accustomed to, they are definitely increasing in popularity with exhibitors and spectators alike. The uninformed public can quickly relate to jumpers as opposed to other horse show classes as the competition is obvious—the results depending upon performance and a numerical score, not opinion. Either the horse gets over the jump or he doesn't, and it is apparent from round to round, even fence to fence, who is in line for the top honours.

For the Jumper Division the obstacles are generally taller and wider than hunter fences and, rather than being natural in appearance, are often brightly coloured. Common jumps to see are slats, panel, barrels, triple bars, and many combinations (two or more fences in a row at related distances). In a hunter class a square oxer is not allowed (the front element of the spread must be at least slightly lower than the back), but this parallel fence is a familiar and challenging jumper obstacle. Unlike the hunters, who are shown braided, a jumper may have a natural mane and tail, though the mane should be neatly pulled short.

The old approach to jumpers is, thankfully, nearly obsolete. In good competition today it is rare that the horse who can just get over the obstacles but us poorly trained will win. The best course designers use all sorts of methods to ensure that the good horse, the one that is balanced and obedient, will win. Height is no longer the only consideration. A top horse must be scopy—that is, capable of changing, lengthening and shortening his stride within seconds, of staying balanced in all sorts of situations and turns, and of handling height and width from a variety of angles. One design is to face the horse with a high vertical that requires some sort of collection after he has just extended himself in clearing a water jump. Another test would be a triple combination, where the horse is allowed one long stride to the second fence but must then shorten quickly, without losing momentum, to handle the third element only two short strides away. Impulsion and balance are the key to success and in the timed jump-offs it is sometimes the horse who can turn and jump, rather than the one who can run and jump, that will win.

Whereas a hunter will usually have fairly good conformation and a daisy-cutter stride, the jumper may move with more knee action and be less classic in build and style. It is rare, though, that the good show jumper does not have at least the essential basics of good conformation. Important are a good shoulder and hock, and strong sound legs. Most jumpers start their days in the Hunter Division, gaining experience over the lower fences. While some horses can move from the Hunter to Jumper Division with ease, there are others who are superb at 3ft 6in and maybe 4ft fences, whose style and ability seem impeccable, but do not have the heart for the big sticks — very often only time will tell.

As the jumper is judged solely on his ability to clear the fences and not on his style, there are successful horses in this division who jump with inverted backs or without really snapping their knees up. The majority however are good jumpers as they must all be true athletes to handle today's big courses. A horse who really uses himself puts out less effort, and thus stays fresher longer, than one who does not.

Grand Prix events

A great boost to the jumper scene has been the introduction of Grand Prix events held over courses of international size and scope.

Opposite Legs should be carefully rinsed and dried, particularly the heels, to prevent soreness and cracking.

Overleaf top When fitting a stable or travelling bandage, the gamgee, used to give extra protection against knocking in a box or stable, is put on under the bandage.

Overleaf below The bandage is applied with the end sticking up, on the second turn the end is folded down, to prevent it slipping.

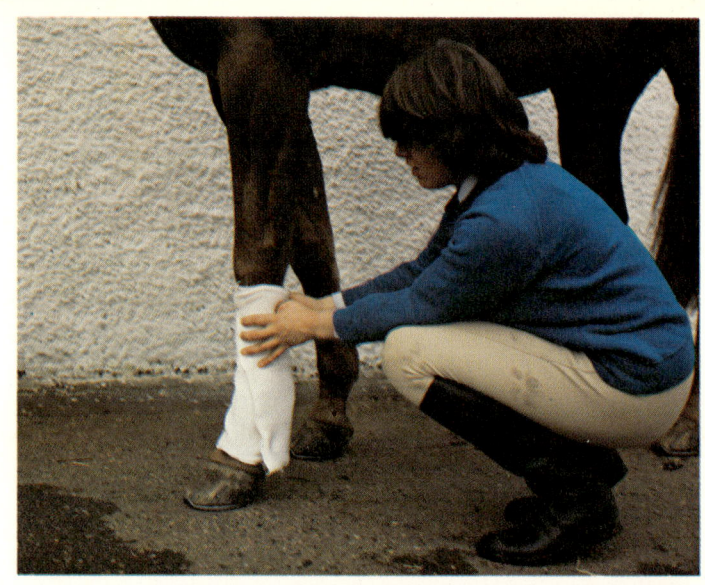
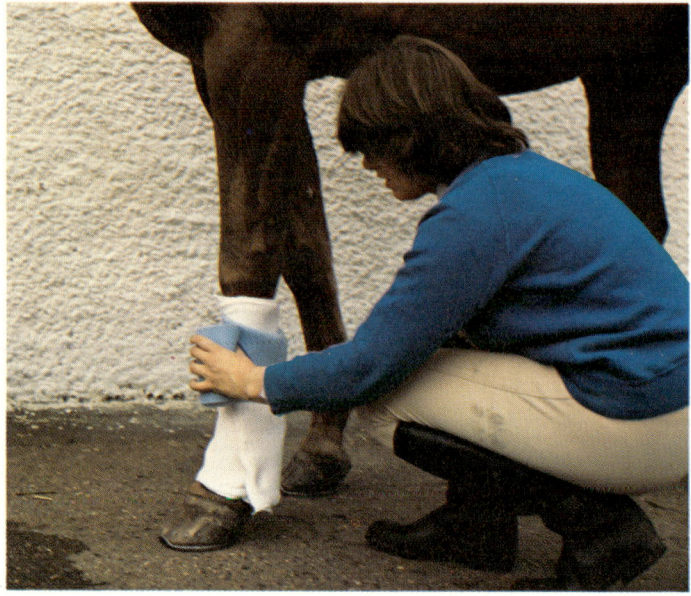

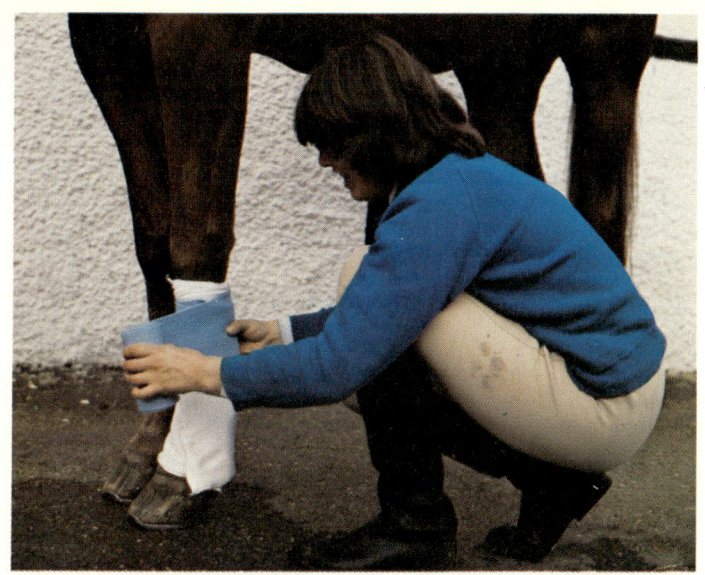
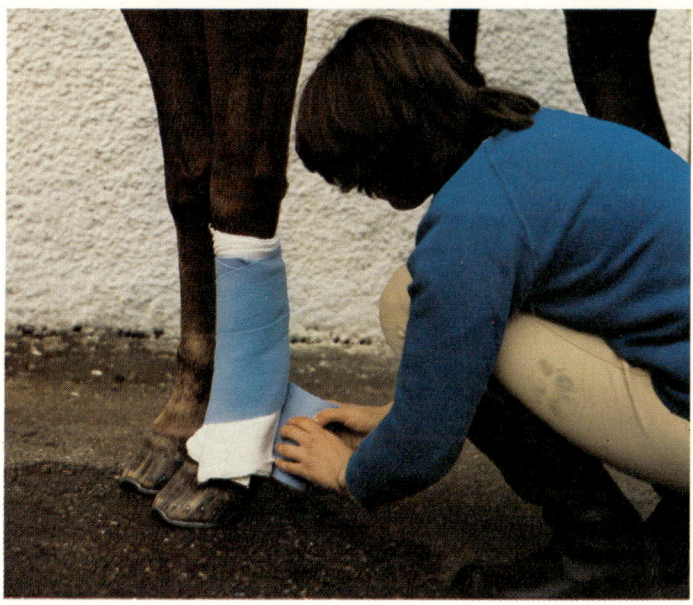

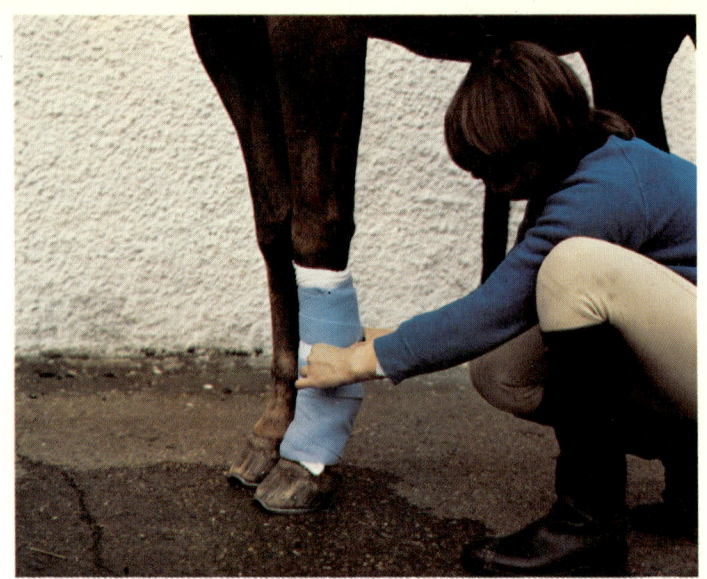
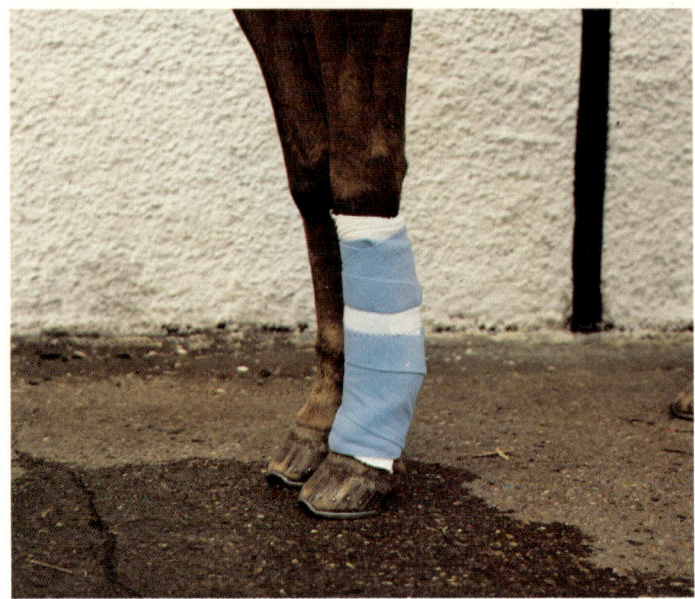

These Grand Prix competitions have been organized with the public in mind. The prize money is attractive enough to make it worthwhile for the top horses and riders to travel and compete and the courses are eye-catching in design. The water jump, that at first caused great controversy with its appearance on the American scene because few horses were used to it, is now an accepted crowd-pleaser and the Grand Prix events are sometimes set up in stadiums at weekends with the intention of drawing big crowds. Slowly, television coverage is being extended and more Americans are accepting show-jumping as an exciting spectator sport.

The normal progression for a Grand Prix prospect is to start out over the low hunter fences and then to move from the Preliminary and Intermediate into the Open Jumper Divisions. These are restricted according to a horse's previous winnings and the highest prize money is always offered in the Open classes. Again, it is important not to upgrade a horse until he is ready for the higher fence heights and stiffer competition of the next rank.

Smaller events

While Grand Prix events are conducted under the international rules of the FEI (Fédération Equestre Internationale), where only knockdowns (not ticks or touchs) are faulted, together with other acts such as refusals and runouts, most smaller events are held under AHSA rules, which vary according to the table and section designated in the prize-lists of each show. A full explanation of scoring procedures is outlined in the AHSA Rulebook but, briefly, in a rub class, the following holds:

Front tick:	1 fault
Hind tick:	½ fault

Previous page (top) As the bandage is put on, each turn round the leg should be even.

Previous page (below) It is important that the bandage is taken right into the heels so that there is less risk of the horse injuring himself.

Opposite top The bandage is taken over the heels and brought evenly up the leg and secured by Velcro fastening.

Opposite below The finished bandage will give warmth and protection to the leg.

First refusal:	3 faults
Second refusal:	6 faults
Third refusal:	Elimination
Knockdown:	4 faults
Front and hind tick (on same fence):	1 fault
Circling (except at the beginning):	3 faults

Although the initial round is not usually against the clock, there is often a time allowed in non-rub classes. Time allowed is a limit that you cannot exceed without incurring extra penalty points: ¼ fault for each second over or fraction thereof. The time is taken from the moment the horse first passes between the start-

Aslan and Helen Gould clearing a 6 foot 6 inch wall to win the puissance class at the National Western Stock Show.

ing markers on the approach to the first fence to when he passes between those on the landing side of the last jump. As a word of caution, never start your round until the whistle blows or you may get eliminated.

In most classes where a two or more way tie for first place exists, there is a jump-off, often with the fences raised and perhaps over a shortened course. If this jump-off is against the clock, which it usually is, it is always the horse with the least faults who will win. Only if two or more have an equal number, or lack of faults does time come into consideration. Obviously the last rider to jump off is at a great advantage, since if all previous riders have faults he can take the risk of going slower and trying to go clear.

Puissance classes

Apart from the Grand Prix, which are often events by themselves, the Puissance classes at regular horse shows, are probably the most exciting jumper competitions for spectators. It is here that ability to clear a high fence is rewarded. The horses start over about six fences until the numbers are reduced in successive jump-offs to two: a spread and a vertical. The vertical is usually the familiar wall that looms higher and higher until finally only one competitor is able to clear it. It is quite usual for heights to range between 6 and 7 feet in the final rounds, when even a brave pair of ears are barely visible to spectators on the landing side!

9 Western riding and stock seat equitation

Stock seat equitation, and the dedication with which it is pursued, belies the casual remark that anybody can ride Western. It is certainly easier to stay aboard in a Western saddle, where one can hang onto the horn for balance, but staying aboard and riding are two entirely different things; to produce a top performance out of a sensitive and responsive stock horse is a fine skill.

There are two basic Western schools in the United States today: the one more prevalent east of the Rockies uses split reins and grazing-type bits such as light curbs; the California school uses connected reins and a romal, and the bits popular with this style are usually heavier and more decorated.

Appointments are important in many Western classes, particularly the equitation. Riders must wear a Western hat, long-sleeved shirt, appropriate neckwear, cowboy boots and chaps. Spurs are optional. The fit of saddle to rider is heavily criticized and, as in hunt and saddle seat classes, certainly affects the rider's performance. For riders using closed reins, hobbles must be carried on the near side of the saddle below the cantle, and all riders must carry a lariat or reata. Silver equipment is becoming increasingly popular but technically it must not receive any precedence over a good working equipment except in parade classes, where appointments count twenty-five per cent rather than the emphasis being almost entirely on performance.

Equitation, pleasure and trail classes

The usual age divisions for equitation are eleven and under, twelve to fourteen, and fifteen to seventeen years old. All contestants are required to show on the rail at a walk, jog, and lope in both directions. The judge may then require two or more additional

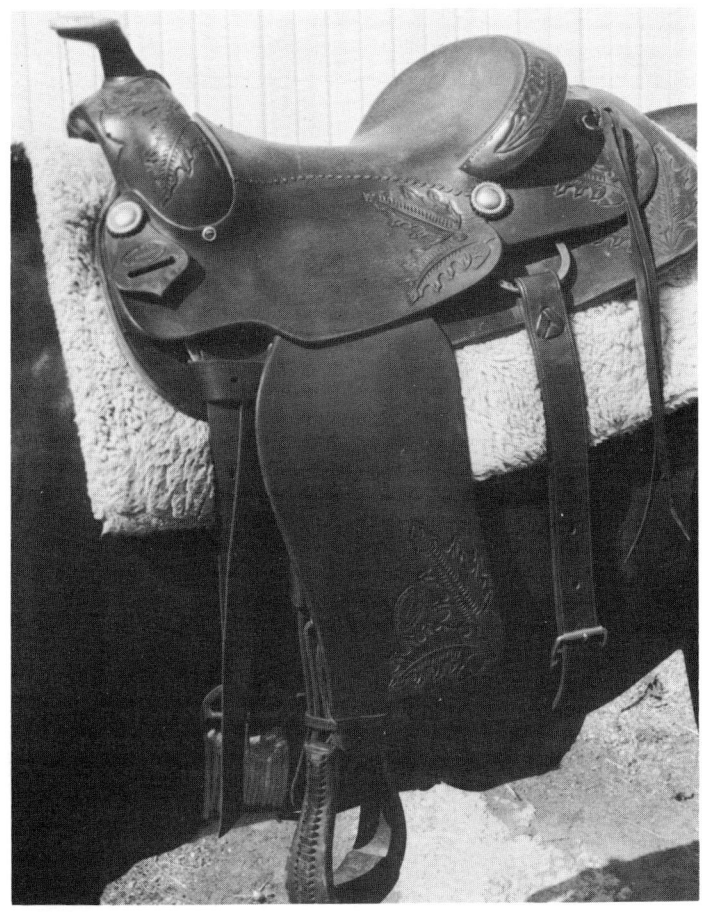

A stock seat or 'Western' saddle from Texas. Note the back cinch that is snugly attached for roping cattle.

tests from those recommended by the AHSA. The eleven and unders may be asked for test 1 to 3 (individual performance on the rail; figure eight at the jog; and lope and stop); the twelve to fourteen year-olds may also be asked for test 4 and 5 (figure eight at a lope with a simple change of lead; ride without stirrups); and in the fifteen to seventeen and open classes, tests 6 to 12 may also be requested (dismount and mount; figure eight at a lope with flying change of lead; change of lead down centre of ring using simple changes; ride a serpentine course demonstrating flying changes; sliding stop; execute 360º turns and spins; and roll backs). The AHSA Medal class is intended to be judged as an open stock horse class, but with the emphasis upon the rider and the methods he uses to obtain his horse's performance rather than upon the performance itself. Rather than just one or two tests, a whole pattern is required.

The complete riding stock horse pattern upon which the Medal workouts are based is fully described in the Rulebook; it can only be perfected by constant practice and observation. Basically it consists of two figure eights, demonstrating flying changes

A Quarter horse in a stock seat equitation class.

The Pinto has a reputation for toughness and endurance and is now used extensively as an all-round horse.

of lead, a gallop the full length of the arena to a sliding stop, a straight and fairly rapid back for 10 - 15ft and a half-turn in each direction. Riders are also sometimes required to perform full and one and a half turns.

In all equitation classes, and particularly in the complicated Medal workout, the horse should be working off his haunches and be quick and responsive to the rider's aids. Again, the ideal is the working stock horse, who must be catlike and always entirely balanced to perform his tasks. A good rider will be able to produce this top performance from his horse while remaining quiet, poised, and subtle in his direction.

Most equitation riders also show in the pleasure division, and those with registered horses compete in their respective breed divisions. By far the most popular stock seat equitation mount is the American Quarter Horse, but, according to regional and personal preference, Arabians, Morgans, Appaloosas, Paints, Pintos and Palominos are also successfully used. It is possible, of course, for an animal to be registered both with the AQHA (American Quarter Horse Association) and the Palomino registry.

A Palomino Quarter horse. These horses are reputed to be versatile, gentle, intelligent and sure-footed.

In pleasure classes personal preference is a heavy factor in the judge's decision. All horses, however, should move in a relaxed manner with a good headset and no fussing at the mouth or head tossing. The stride should be ground-covering and appear fluid and effortless. Obviously, the horse should be in balance and obedient at all times and every entry should be able to stand quietly in the line up and to back readily upon request.

Trail classes are popular with all ages and provide spectators with some excitement after the pleasure and equitation classes, which require a more informed audience. Generally the whole class begins by working on the rail in both directions before competitors proceed individually through the obstacle course. The course varies from show to show, and when held in an arena will be restricted in the kind of natural obstacles it can set up — such as water and riding into and out of a ditch. The most common tests are to open and close a gate while mounted, cross a bridge, back through an obstacle requiring a turn, and to carry articles from one point to another. As preparation for this class the horse should be accustomed to strange sights and sounds and should, as much as possible, rehearse the expected tests. It is important that the horse's attention always be focused on the rider, not just on the obstacle at hand, and there should never appear to be any hesitation in his performance.

Pleasure, equitation and trail classes are for some exhibitors only a beginning, the first step towards developing their skills to show successfully a reining horse or working stock horse.

Reining classes

In reining classes, contestants must ride a prescribed pattern demonstrating the partnership between rider and horse. The performance should be fluid and accurate, with the rider giving subtle aids and remaining always in control. The horse should respond quickly and perform without hesitation or anticipation. To avoid the appearance of a rehearsed performance, it is important in training not to put the whole routine together too frequently. The figure eights may be practised, the turns, the runs and the sliding stops, but they should rarely be put together in the correct sequence if anticipation is to be avoided. Throughout the performance the horse should appear responsive, light in the bridle, balanced with his feet under him, and working with his mouth closed.

Working stock horse classes

In contrast to the reining class, where a good deal of emphasis inevitably falls upon accuracy of the pattern executed and sublety of the rider, the working stock horse classes are focused almost entirely upon the horse. Exhibitors are usually required to work first as a group on the rail and then individually to ride a pattern similar to that of the reining class. The second part of the class involves actually working a cow. Each entry works alone in the arena with the cow, turning and circling it according to the judge's orders. Points are awarded on a scale from 60 to 80 with a score of 70 indicating an average performance.

Cutting Horse Contest

Perhaps the ultimate in Western riding is the Cutting Horse Contest, operating under the rules of the National Cutting Horse Association (NCHA, PO Box 12155, 4704 Benbrook Highway, Fort Worth, Texas 76116). This is the *haute école* of Western riding, where the horse appears almost to dance, so lithe and graceful are his movements. The contest consists of working a group of cattle and cutting one cow from the group. An experienced cow horse works largely on its own initiative, sitting way back on its haunches and pivoting its forelegs from side to side one moment, then putting on a short burst of speed to shadow the cow the next. The horse will learn to anticipate the cow's every move and respond accordingly until, triumphant, horse and rider have defied the cow's strongest instinct and separated him from the herd. In teaching a youngster, or sharpening up an experienced cutting horse, some trainers employ a mechanical cow. This machine, which can turn, spin and run on remote control, allows the rider with the help of his ground man to repeat manoeuvres that his horse finds especially hard.

10 The American Saddlebred

The American Saddle Horse has often been called the peacock of the show ring. In 1891 the first Saddle Horse Breeders Association was formed in Louisville, Kentucky, the heart of Saddler country. Originating from the comfortable plantation horses of the 1800s, the breed has been carefully developed to produce its animated performers.

Its conformation makes possible the extreme collection and animation of a top show horse. Without a fine throttle and long crested neck that blends with good sloping shoulders, the fine headset — that distinguishing trait of the Saddlebred — would not be possible. The front end should be topped by a fine boned head that presents a straight profile, perhaps slightly Roman nosed in a few individuals, but never concave. The back should be fairly short with a level croup and high-set tail, and the wide-girthed body should be set upon straight legs with sloping pasterns. The hind legs are very important as they support almost the entire movement of the horse.

Saddlebred divisions

Depending upon conformation and ability, the Saddle-horse destined for the show ring may be produced for one of three major divisions: Three-gaited, Five-gaited or Fine Harness.

The three-gaited horses are known as 'walk-trotters' as their main gait is the striking park trot. The best conformation horses are usually found in these classes, which are divided according to height: 15.2 hands and under, and over 15.2 hands. As with the Five-Gaited and Fine Harness Divisions, there are also junior exhibitor and lady or amateur classes. The walk-trot horses are in fact exhibited at the walk, trot and canter.

The five-gaited horses are probably the most renowned of the Saddlebreds as they exhibit the famous artificial gaits, the rack and slow gait. Their speciality is the style and speed at which they show. The trot and rack are the gaits at which most speed is called for, but it must never be developed at the sacrifice of form. The rack (which is a high-action, four-beat gait with the feet striking the ground in the following order: right hind, right front, left hind, left front) requires a great deal of stamina and it is not unusual for a five-gaiter to be slightly heavier in bone than the walk-trotter. As there is a great chance of the hind foot striking the front at an extended rack, it is important that the horse wear protective quarter-boots on his front hooves. Not only is the chance of injury lessened but the horse will not be afraid to extend for fear of hurting himself. The slow gait is animated yet slow, and in contrast to the rack, there is much less tension on the reins. Five-gaited horses are shown according to their age and sex, not height.

In the Fine Harness Division it is not unusual to see some younger horses. Some trainers prefer to produce their young stock first in harness and then later move them into the three and five-gaited classes. Although a horse can be moved directly to the Three-Gaited Division after showing in harness, the five-gaited prospects often spend a period out of the show ring while in training - otherwise they might get excited or confused and try racking in harness! There are horses who will remain in harness, as their fine conformation and excellent trots may be most appreciated while put to a buggy. The trot of the harness horse is his forte, and without the encumbrance of a rider the animals can really show off. Extreme speed may be penalized and the driver must be able to maintain the gait and control of the buggy while executing turns and staying clear of other contestants. An appropriate vehicle is required (usually a small, easily manoeuvred buggy with four wire wheels), the horse must use light harness with a snaffle bit and overcheck, and should be shown with a full mane and tail.

An excellent starting place for the Saddlebred amateur is the newer and increasingly popular Pleasure Horse Division. Open only to amateur or junior riders or drivers, the classes are judged seventy-five per cent on manners, performance and ability to give a good pleasure ride, and only twenty-five per cent on conformation and neatness of attire. Here the less expensive horse with a conscientious rider can really succeed, and the rider gain valuable show ring miles. The pleasure Saddlebred, under English or Western tack, must be shown with a full mane and tail, and the tail should not have been set in preparation for the current show. Gingering is prohibited. The horses show at a walk, trot and canter and must be able to stand quietly and rein back readily.

Saddlebred training

The education of a Saddlebred for the ring is an art that has often been abused, creating a sometimes infamous reputation for the breed. There have been many methods of getting these horses to perform, but the top trainers' approaches are designed to enhance the natural tendencies of the animal and their techniques are rarely the inhumane atrocities attributed to them.

The young horse should be accustomed gradually to the full show bridle. The eventual action of the curb and snaffle that produces the fine headset of the more mature Saddlebred is probably best introduced by the use of a simple snaffle bridle with two reins — the bottom one passing through a running martingale that only approximates the leverage action that the curb will have. Great attention must be given to developing a good mouth and headset because, without them, true collection is impossible to attain.

Shoeing by an experienced farrier can definitely affect a horse's way of going. Critics have complained about the long feet of the Saddlebred, but a good shoer, by judicious use of weights and by varying the length of foot, can enhance a horse's natural way of going without causing the animal discomfort. As another aid to improve action it is a familiar training sight to see 'rattlers' around the horse's pastern — chains used to encourage him to lift his feet. Any schooling technique, however, can only improve upon a horse's natural tendencies, not change them, and all are to no avail if the basic head carriage and collection have not already been achieved by patient training.

The two controversial habits of gingering and 'breaking the horse's tail' are probably the most misunderstood of Saddlebred mysteries. Gingering is the practice of inserting an irritant in the horse's rectum before a class to keep his tail held high and straight. The trainer should know just how much irritant is needed to maintain the tail set for a class and also how long it will take to have effect — at once or only after several minutes. 'Breaking the horse's tail', the operation performed to make it easier for the horses to carry their tails in the unnaturally high position common to show horses, does not actually involve breaking the tail. The depressor muscles that hold the horse's tail down are cut and, if properly cared for, there are usually no post-operative complications. It is essential to the horse's comfort however that the tailsetter, designed to hold the horse's tail in the desired position while not in the show ring, is used and adjusted correctly. It is most important that anyone who is inexperienced should not attempt tailsetting without expert supervision. In addition to setting the tails, some exhibitors add supplementary hair to the mane and tail.

The fieriness of the Saddlebred in the show ring should not be encouraged at the expense of either manners or form. To create a top performer it is essential never to allow the animal to change gaits or switch rhythms without a direct signal from the rider. To be present at the American Royal in Kansas City, the Chicago International, the Kentucky State Fair in Louisville, or the Garden and to thrill to the cry of 'Rack on!' is for many the ultimate in appreciating the American Saddle Horse.

11 The Morgan

Compact could be the word used to describe Vermont's state animal, the Morgan Horse. This small yet elegant breed usually stands about 14.1 to 15.1 hands, and is unique in that all its horses are descended from a single foundation sire, Justin Morgan.

The distinctive head of the Morgan is wide-browed with large generous eyes. A fine throttle places it upon a well-crested neck, whose topline should blend imperceptibly with the withers. Neither too prominent, not too flat, the withers should be well behind the front legs, making for a short back. The croup should be quite long and level with a high-set tail. The legs should be squarely under the horse and characteristically be well-muscled above the knee and hock. Despite his compactness, the show Morgan is a refined creature.

The Morgan.

As with the Saddlebred, whose neck is also set well over the shoulders, headset is essential in developing the balanced and collected way of going that allows for the Morgan's high action. Most people prefer to show in a Weymouth type of full bridle, often sporting a stitched cavesson and a coloured browbrand that may even be co-ordinated with the rider's outfit.

Morgan classes

The Morgan is shown as either a park or a pleasure horse. Park horses are the most animated performers, where height of action is encouraged. They usually enter the ring at a bright trot and the walk is only briefly judged between the trot and canter. The canter should be fluid, collected and slow. The trot is their most distinctive gait and, as with the Saddlebred, the action should be lofty but even. The gait should never deviate from a true two-beat and and the horse should be moving parallel to the rail, not dancing sideways.

The pleasure Morgan also enters the ring at a trot, but although he must be well balanced and obedient he does not display the same kind of animation or action as the park horse. The headset is more relaxed, with less rein contact, and the horse should have ground-covering action, effortless enough to be maintained easily over long periods. The extended or road trot is the gait of the pleasure horse and he should be able to extend smoothly and dramatically with no loss of form while remaining on a fairly relaxed rein. Pleasure horses may also be required to encounter some obstacles, such as cavalletti, a bridge, or a gate, if the prize list has so stipulated. Unlike the park horse who may get away with slight deviations at the walk, the pleasure Morgan must have a square and relaxed walk that would be a pleasure to sit.

Opposite top Divide the mane into even sections, fastened with elastic bands, before starting to braid.

Opposite below Braid each hank of hair, binding the end tightly with cotton and leaving the ends of the cotton free.

Overleaf top Thread the loose ends of cotton through a blunt darning needle, roll up the braids, turning the ends under and sew them up.

Overleaf below Neat braids give your horse a smart appearance for the ring.

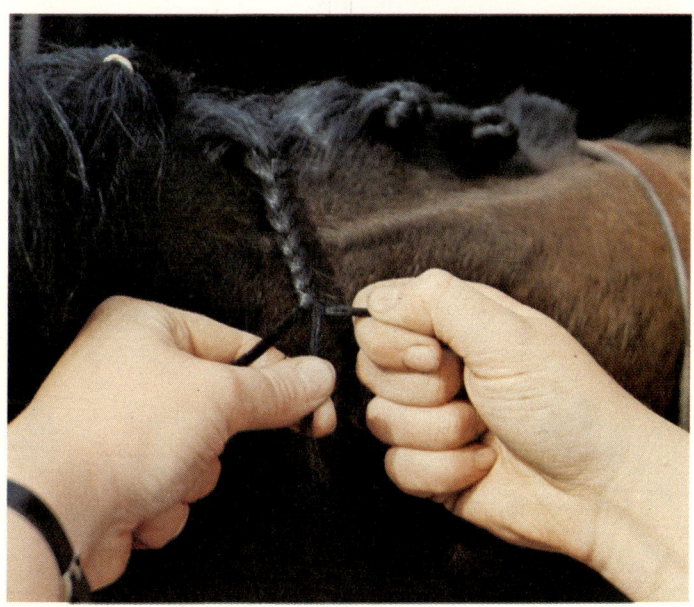

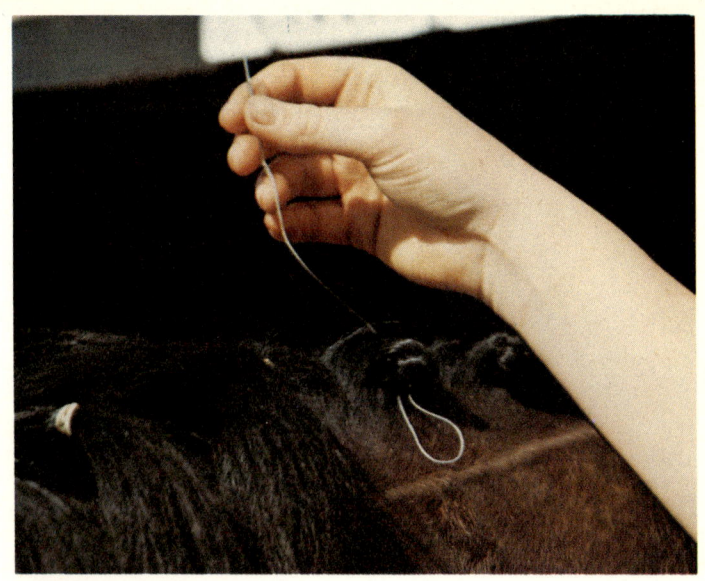

The Pleasure Division may be divided into English and Western classes. Although most English riders prefer to use the cutback saddle, the hunt seat is also correct; the rider's attire must correspond to the tack he has chosen.

The park and pleasure distinction continues into the harness classes, where the Morgan will show either as a park harness or a pleasure driving horse. Conformation is all-important, for only the horse who is built well will look well in harness, and even the more relaxed pleasure horse should carry himself well. The Park Harness Division is similar to the American Saddlebred's fine harness classes, using the same type of four-wheeled vehicles and fancy harness. The park horse's trot should again be flashy and brilliant, and the walk is often judged as the animals reverse through the centre of the ring. Though it should be collected and controlled it need not be a true flat-foot walk.

In the pleasure driving classes the two-wheeled jog-cart has become more popular than the less easily manoeuvred four-wheeled buggy. The cart may be naturally varnished or in the stable colours. The pleasure Morgan, unlike the park harness horse, must exhibit a true flat-foot walk and have excellent manners. As with the pleasure horse under saddle, he should be shown with a more relaxed head carriage than the park horse and must demonstrate effortless ground-covering action. The road trot should be in form and control, and he must stand quietly and back readily.

The Justin Morgan class is intended to demonstrate versitality. The same horse is asked to race a half-mile in harness, then a half-mile under saddle, to show at the walk, trot and canter, and then to be placed in a work harness to drag a stoneboat a required distance.

In keeping with tradition, the Morgan must be shown in his natural glory with no braiding, tailsetting, irritants or other unnatural devices except for moderate length of toe and weights.

Previous page (top) Pulling the horse's mane to thin and shorten it is best done by twisting hair around a mane comb.

Previous page (below) Decorative patterns on the horse's quarters can be made with the help of a mane comb.

Opposite To clean the saddle, remove dirt with a well squeezed out sponge and warm water then apply saddle soap with a nearly-dry sponge.

12 Tennessee Walkers

The Walker has been called the world's greatest pleasure horse, and the distinguishing trait of all members of the breed is the famous running walk. The Walker appears powerful yet graceful in build and his conformation must lend itself to the tremendous amount of push required from the hind legs and the capacity to pull and reach with the front. His long neck is set onto a short back, deep at the girth, with a sloping croup.

The Tennessee Walking Horse was originally bred as an all-round working horse, but became famous for its smooth gaits.

The running walk is a free and gliding gait, lofty in action, and ground-covering in scope. Its most remarkable feature is the tremendous overstride displayed by a good horse — as much as 12 to 30in! It must be particularly straight in action and contain no hesitant or twisting motion. The regular walk should be flat-footed and the canter a rocking-chair gait, with pronounced natural head motion and a rolling stride, with knee and hock action comparable.

The practice of 'soring' Walking Horses was throughout the sixties an issue of heated controversy. It had been the method of many trainers to apply certain substances around the coronet area to produce a great deal of irritation or soreness which would cause the horse to become exaggerated in his action. Fortunately, this has now been thoroughly outlawed by both the government and by horse associations. Breeders need no longer worry that unnatural movers may win in the show ring because of soring practices, and the AHSA is very firm in its support and supervision of the protective rules.

In certain classes action devices, such as smooth chains around the pastern, are permitted, but whenever boots are worn the judges must request removal of at least one of them to inspect it carefully for any illegal action-producing devices. To guard against soring outside the show ring, the AHSA Rulebook also stipulates the following: 'Horses foaled after 1 January 1972 with any bilateral scar, callous, or granulated tissue on the pastern or coronet areas indicative of soring are not eligible to be shown in any Walking Horse performance class'.

Walker classes

One of the most popular Walker classes has always been one where soring was never really necessary — the Plantation class. Here the Walkers perform in their natural magnificence — not even hoof bands are permitted — and they are judged as a true pleasure ride that would be fit for plantation and trail use. Horses shown in this class must also be shod with a regular, unweighted shoe.

Perhaps the most colourful class at Walking Horse shows is the Southern Belle Walk. Restricted to ladies only, this event requires entrants to wear antebellum costume and show their mounts side-saddle. It serves as a great reminder of the Walker's past as a plantation horse of the old South.

The Walker in action. Characteristic of the breed is the long head, pointed ears, powerful neck, sloping shoulder and short back.

13 The Quarter Horse

The American Quarter Horse is so named because of his unbeatable prowess in races at a quarter-mile distance. As far back as 1665 the American Quarter Running Horse was recognized, long before the importation of English Thoroughbred blood. His powerful hindquarters are his striking trait, and have been put to many uses in his role as a stock, jumping and race horse. These quarters are set upon a powerful yet elegant body, which is closely coupled

Australians have taken enthusiastically to breeding quarter-horses. Here is a fine example.

with a deep girth and set upon strong legs with heavily muscled forearms and gaskins and short cannons. The head has a wide jaw, tapering to a shapely muzzle and the eyes are wide-set and generous. Small ears are placed in front of the shapely throttle that joins the head to a crested, muscled, and often fairly short neck.

The horse described is the traditional stock type of Quarter Horse, but the tremendous variety of strains and all the attempts to infuse racing blood for speed have produced many leggy and more lightly built Quarter Horses that very closely resemble the Thoroughbred. It is often these lithe yet tractable creatures who excel in racing and show-jumping where a longer leg and stride is appreciated. A Thoroughbred-Quarter cross often produces many of the Thoroughbred's physical characteristics, complemented by sensible Quarter Horse temperament.

The American Quarter horse, with characteristic short head, powerful quarters, strong back, sloping shoulder and well-muscled forelegs.

Starting in 1940, long after the origins of Quarter Horse history, the American Quarter Horse Association established its registry and has since made tremendous strides in documenting and regulating Quarter Horse bloodlines. The AQHA is the parent body of the many smaller Quarter Horse associations scattered around the country, and has been very influential in the development of the breed as we know it today. Its headquarters are in the cow country state, Texas (PO Box 200, Amarillo, Texas 79105) and everyone intending to compete in Quarter Horse competitions should definitely read their official handbook.

As has already been mentioned, the Quarter Horse excels in the stock-horse arena, leading the field in working cowhorse, reining and cutting-horse competitions. He is also at the top in calf-roping and rodeo events and surpasses every other breed in open competition for the first choice in Western pleasure and stock seat equitation classes.

The AQHA, in its efforts to refine and develop the breed as a performance horse, has established two Registers of Merit — one for working events and one for racing. There are three major degrees awarded: the Register of Merit, the AQHA Champion, and ultimately, the AQHA Supreme Champion. To become eligible for a given title a horse must win a certain number of points in various performance fields. The points must be earned in classes limited to AQHA registered horses in the following areas: racing; reining; working cowhorse, western riding; barrel racing; pole bending; jumping, working hunter, polo; western pleasure, trail horse, English pleasure and calf roping, steer roping, cutting. Points are awarded not only according to how a horse places but to how many exhibitors it has competed against to win. For example, if there are only five to nine entries in a class the winner would receive only one point for the blue whereas, in a large class of thirty or more exhibitors, the winner would receive six points and the sixth placing horse would even receive one.

Although he has always been the undisputed king as a stock horse, the lighter weight, long-legged Quarter Horse and Quarter Horse cross are becoming increasingly popular in the hunter and jumper arena.

14 The Appaloosa

The Appaloosa has a romantic past tracing all the way back to the Ice Age. Throughout history the spotted horse has appeared in various works of art and has been favoured as the steed of kings and emperors. The American Appaloosa is directly descended from the horse the Spaniards brought with them when they conquered Mexico and California. Subsequently the Nez Percé Indians made use of the breed, and in turn, when the United States cavalry moved in, it became crossed with ranch and work-

The Appaloosa with mottled skin, white sclera surrounding the eyes and striped hooves.

horse blood. Not until early this century were attempts made to improve and refine the breed. In 1938 the Appaloosa Horse Club made its small beginning, and now it is able to be selective in its registry. The Club's headquarters are in Idaho (PO Box 403, Moscow, Idaho 83843) and all horses exhibiting in Appaloosa classes at recognized shows must be registered.

Owners and breeders are quick to point out that the Appaloosa is identified by far more than just his colour. There are certain physical breed characteristics that distinguish the horse. Most striking is the white sclera around the eye; the hoof is usually vertically striped; the skin is mottled — a trait that should always be evident in the genital region; the tail and mane are often sparse; and some horses have what are referred to as varnish marks — groupings of dark hair on certain parts of the body. In registering an Appaloosa six main colour patterns are recognized: the spotted blanket; white blanket; leopard; snowflake; frost; and marble. Marginal horses are ones which lack distinctive colouring, and they should be especially strong in physical characteristics.

At Appaloosa shows there are Hunt Seat and Western Divisions, often with classes over fences for hunters and jumpers. Annually there is a National Appaloosa Horse Show with exhibitors travelling from many states to compete. It is not unusual to see the Appaloosa in his element at major all-breed shows as a stock or reining horse in the open events, and then also competing in the calf-roping and reining classes of the Appaloosa Division. The most colourful class for spectators is the Nez Pérce Stake Race. Contestants must wear historical costume relating to the Appaloosa's past. The riders, disguised as kings, emperors, Indians and Conquistadores, race two at a time on adjacent six-stake courses until, after winner plays winner, a final victor emerges!

The minimum height for the Appaloosa is 14 hands, but there is a whole miniature or pony division, recognized as a separate breed, Ponies of the Americas, (POA, PO Box 1447, Mason City, Iowa 50401). These ponies must have an official measurement card and are supposed to display a mixture of Arabian and Quarter Horse blood with Appaloosa colouring. Their maximum height is 13.2 hands.

15 Riding side-saddle

Nowhere at a show is there a more elegant and graceful sight than the side-saddle class, which is now growing enormously in popularity.

Before entering for a side-saddle class yourself it will be well worth while to go to an expert for advice and a few lessons. Ideally, the horse you learn on should already be accustomed to being ridden side-saddle. You will probably want to ride side-saddle for the very best reason that it does look so beautiful, so you want to do it correctly. Riding side-saddle is not, in fact, at all difficult — but it will feel a bit different the first time you try! You always have to be given a leg-up into the saddle so remember, in the show ring, to have some one suitable on hand. He will be needed after your horse has been individually led out in hand for the judge.

A side-saddle is designed to be ridden on the left side and it has two pommels, over one of which the rider rests her right leg, placing the left leg under the lower pommel. The seat is often made of doeskin. It is essential to have a saddle that fits your mount properly; on some ponies a balance strap is helpful to prevent slipping. Older saddles have out-of-date safety fittings and it may be impossible to find suitable stirrup leather fittings.

Once in the saddle, you will find that you are really sitting on your right buttock only! What is more, you will convey most of the aids with your seat, so it is essential to have a well-schooled horse. There will be no leg aids on the right-hand side, although a tap with a long stick may be given if necessary.

The first thing to remember is to keep your right shoulder well back because this keeps you straight in the saddle. Your hands should be held low and not, as is all too often seen, clutching the reins above the wither as if hanging on to a bunch of

The correct position in a side-saddle, shown without the skirt. It is surprisingly secure as long as the right shoulder is kept back.

knitting! Add to the grace by sitting upright with a straight back, stomach muscles in, but do not stiffen — relax yourself, and your horse will not tense up either. It is surprising how secure you will feel no matter what mischief your horse gets up to, so long as you remember to keep that right shoulder back. Do not attempt to rise at the trot, as a sitting trot is used in side-saddle riding; you will even be more comfortable at the canter, flowing over the ground in complete unison with your horse.

Side-saddle hack class

The side-saddle hack class often brings a change of form from astride classes, as a larger made hack with a longer back and low stride has a tendency to give a more comfortable side-saddle ride than a more compact little horse. The class is judged as in other hack classes but, besides the ride side-saddle, the judge is looking for the hack that goes smoothly and easily for the rider. This requires a higher standard of training than with astride riding and here the older, more experienced hack has an advantage over the younger horse. You need to be able to convey to the horse with the slightest movement what you want him to do, and this can be practised astride at home until perfected.

Side-saddle on a pony

Pony side-saddle classes are also judged on the pony's conformation and way of going, although some classes have been introduced where it is the best side-saddle rider that is looked for. This seems a good idea that should further the standard of riding.

A champion side-saddle hack and rider. A larger horse with a long back and low stride, gives a more comfortable ride.

16 Driving at shows

Driving at shows can be a very rewarding experience, particularly when it is realized just how much the watching public appreciates the old-world sight of horses and ponies in harness.

The first item to be considered is how best to travel, for there are several methods. Some people prefer boxing their horse, or horses, in a low-load trailer with the carriage mounted on the towing vehicle. The advantage of this is that everything except the horse can be loaded well in advance. Another method is for both carriage and animals to be carried on separate low-load trailers. A third type of transport can be achieved with a motor horsebox large enough to carry the entire turnout, vehicle and its horse or horses. In bad weather this is ideal, but it is essential to ensure that in an emergency the horse can be unloaded quickly and easily. Apart from the transport of carriage and horse, the harness requires careful packing in containers.

In order to succeed at shows today an extremely high standard must be achieved, so the vehicle and harness should be both painted and polished to maximum effect. In addition to suiting the colour of the vehicle to the horse, the actual types of both should be considered. Stocky ponies need sporty or rustic vehicles while animals with finer limbs require the more elegant phaetons and gigs. Harness, too, should be of correct type for the turnout, rustic vehicles requiring either brown or black leather, while patent leather should be reserved for the smarter vehicles.

Turnout

In addition to the appearance of the horse, which of course must be well-groomed, with its hooves oiled and its mane appropriately taken care of, the outfit of the driver and his attendant groom (who is essential for safety's sake) must also be considered. Elegance, not flashiness, is the goal. Fancy dress or period costume should not be worn except when appearing in displays or pageants, or events such as the Cavalcade Americana class. An apron and gloves should be worn by both sexes. The whip must be carried at all times in order to urge on, correct, or possibly to distract the horse in an emergency.

At the show

Before the start of a class, a short session of warming-up, walking and trotting about the grounds, makes good sense as it will help to calm an over-exuberant horse and also loosens any stiff joints.

The complete turnout of horse, driver and vehicle is of prime importance in show driving events.

It is customary to be lined up for inspection before going out either to do an individual 'show' around the ring, or for the drive on the road. The judge will examine harness for its cleanliness, suppleness and fit. Vehicles are looked at not only for their appearance but also for their size and suitability for the horse. The horse itself is judged firstly on conformation – its most important attributes being depth of heart and the possession of a 'leg at each corner' ending in good feet which are well shod. Its action, which need not be exaggerated but should be free and flowing, is noted, but above all its manners are important, so that even with courage and presence it is both obedient and suitable for an amateur to drive. Judges also often ask to see what spares are carried, as these are important when going out on the road.

In the road section, judges usually try to conceal themselves at strategic points so that, unseen, they can gain a better idea of the horses' performances than in the ring. Then, on their return, they examine them for fitness – excessive sweating, for example, will lose marks.

Back in the ring again, the atmosphere becomes really tense when driving round for the final selection. It is now that drivers should proceed with extra caution, for it must be remembered that other competitors may be having problems to cope with, trying to hold back an over-keen horse or perhaps to push on a reluctant one. In all cases, it is wise to steer very clear of other turnouts. Rushing past too closely is more likely to cause an upset of some sort. It is best to hold well back, even to slow down at corners, in order to give your horse a clear run down the side of the ring.

After the class has finished, do not remove the bridle until the horse is free from the vehicle. This is potentially extremely dangerous and many accidents have been caused this way The proper procedure is first always to undo the breeching straps, then to remove the traces, unbuckle the belly band, and then, with an assistant, lead the horse away from the vehicle. Only then can his bridle be replaced by a headcollar with safety.

American classes are often offered according to breed, and may have park or fine harness or pleasure driving classes. In park and fine harness classes brilliance and conformation count heavily, whereas in pleasure classes the judge is looking for ground-covering action and a true pleasure driving horse. There are also roadster classes, in which the standardbred horse, bred for his trotting speed, excels. The main gait for Roadsters is the trot at three speeds: the slow jog trot, the fast road gait and full speed. Even at full speed the horse is expected to maintain good collection. Perhaps the most interesting driving competitions of all are the three-day events run under FEI rules, with three consecutive days of various driving manoeuvres — a dressage drive, endurance drive, and an obstacle course with turns and figures to be executed — to decide the final victor.

In the Roadster class, the standardbred horse shows off its trotting speeds.